THE RULES

To Daisy

First published in Great Britain in 2022 by

Policy Press, an imprint of
Bristol University Press
University of Bristol
1-9 Old Park Hill
Bristol
BS2 8BB
UK
t: +44 (0)117 374 6645
e: bup-info@bristol.ac.uk

Details of international sales and distribution partners are available at
policy.bristoluniversitypress.co.uk

British Library Cataloguing in Publication Data
A catalogue record for this book is available from the British Library

ISBN 978-1-4473-6414-6 paperback
ISBN 978-1-4473-6415-3 ePub
ISBN 978-1-4473-6416-0 ePdf

The right of Marcial Bragadini Bóo to be identified as author of this work has been
asserted by him in accordance with the Copyright, Designs and Patents Act 1988.

The statements and opinions contained within this publication are solely those of
the author and not of the University of Bristol or Bristol University Press. The
University of Bristol and Bristol University Press disclaim responsibility for any injury
to persons or property resulting from any material published in this publication.

Bristol University Press and Policy Press work to counter discrimination on grounds
of gender, race, disability, age and sexuality.

Cover design: James Hepworth
Front cover image: James Hepworth

Bristol University Press and Policy Press use
environmentally responsible print partners.

Printed and bound in Great Britain by TJ Books, Padstow

THE RULES OF DEMOCRACY

Marcial Bragadini Bóo

Contents

Acknowledgements

I am grateful to Stuart Reid and Gill Raikes for their encouragement at the beginning of this project, and to them and Alex Oliver, Alexander Stevenson, Antonia Gracie, Benoit Guerin, Enrique Bóo, Ian Kennedy, Matthew Flinders, Nick Pearce, Nick Sharman, Ruth Knox, Sebastian Bóo and Vicky Fox for their grace in reading and commenting on an early draft. I thank Nick Pearce, Matthew Flinders and Sonny Leong for putting me in touch with Policy Press, and Rebecca Tomlinson, Freya Trand and Caroline Astley at the Press, as well as their anonymous reviewers and the freelance copyeditor, Dawn Rushen, for helping me to transform the material into something readable. Later helpful comments were made by Anthony Barker, Andreas Bummel, Oonagh Gay, Lauren Martin, John Vlasto, Brian Walker and Tony Wright, to whom I am very grateful. All errors are mine.

For their influence, and for allowing me to observe at close quarters how they mastered the arts of democracy in practice, I am ever grateful to Tessa Blackstone, David Blunkett, Michael Bichard, Conor Ryan, Michael Barber, Tony Blair, Hilary Benn, John Gieve, Christopher Kelly, Margaret Hodge, Michael Whitehouse, Amyas Morse, Ian Kennedy, Tony Wright, David Natzler, Jeremy Heywood, John Bercow, Charles Walker, Valerie Vaz, Lindsay Hoyle, Jacob Rees-Mogg, Kathryn Stone, Ian Blackford and the many other MPs I have worked with.

Introduction:
Playing by the rules

The COVID-19 pandemic has changed the world. The immediate impact has been felt in lockdowns, lost jobs and lives gone. The social and economic consequences will be felt for decades.

Of the many lessons from COVID-19, one must surely be to find ways to run the world better, so we can make faster, more informed and fairer collective decisions that benefit the most people possible. Political bluster proved no barrier to the pandemic. Many national responses were poorly planned or coordinated, with failures to share information, protective equipment and vaccines. More died than needed to.

But the devastation of the pandemic highlighted an existing problem. Globalisation, and the technological revolution that accompanied it, had already caused major social changes that have worried communities across the world since the 1990s.

Some have been scared that globalisation is damaging the sovereignty and ancient identity of their country. Others are fearful that global trade is destroying their local economy and livelihood. Or that unchecked immigration is overwhelming public services. Or that environmental disaster will destroy the planet. Or that every aspect of life is being monitored by anonymous tech giants. Or that international cyber-criminals are manipulating bank accounts and rigging elections. Or that predatory capitalists are running the world for the benefit of the 1 per cent elite to the detriment of everyone else.

These fears have manifested in the rise of populism and authoritarian leaders, in anti-capitalist and environmental movements, and in conspiracy theories on the dark web. These fears were well captured by the Brexit slogan, recognising that people wanted to 'take back control' over their own lives.

Yet, however varied these fears and those who express them, the concerns share a common feature: there is too large a gap between those who make the decisions that impact on our lives, and us. There is an Accountability Gap. We have little influence over those who run global businesses and technology firms. Over those who damage the environment. Over those who set international trade rules. Over those trying to prevent and stop an invisible virus. In fact, in many cases no one has much influence over these decision-makers at all. They are largely unaccountable. As a consequence, many suspect that these decision-makers are acting only in their own interests, even though their decisions shape how we all live and the future of all our communities.

This lack of control is happening when we have come to expect more from life. Globalisation and the technological revolution have given us instant access to everything. Whether we are travelling on a rural bus or sitting in an urban cafe, we can see a million images of money, glamour and success in our very own hand. We may want that for ourselves and for our children. We may even be prepared to cross oceans to get it. And we may also want for our community the education, health, safety and social support that we see elsewhere, including on streamed films where roads are smooth, schools are well equipped and hospital staff are attractive. Our expectations are now simply higher, and they are not being met. There is an Expectation Gap.

Globalisation and the technological revolution, together referred to here as the Global Technological Revolution, have brought massive improvements to standards of living and the quality of life around the world, just as the Industrial Revolution did 200 years ago. But the Global Technological Revolution has also brought a profound sense of unfairness. An international, one-in-a-thousand, global elite of perhaps 8 million people is benefiting disproportionately, and can protect itself better, financially and physically, against disease, distress and disaster. The remaining 7,692 million people of the world are not benefiting as much. Many think this inequality unfair.

But the way for people to 'take back control' and to have more say in the decisions that affect their lives is not to pretend that the Global Technological Revolution has not happened, to withdraw from international groups, to build walls or to imagine that communities can retreat to a past time of glory. Instead, we can take back control over those who seem out of control or uncontrollable, whether they run global tech firms or our countries, or destroy the environment.

These decision-makers can be more accountable for their decisions through democracy, humanity's most complex social creation. Democracy is the strongest, most effective way to give us control over decisions that impact our lives. Democracy allows us to choose who makes and scrutinises decisions on our behalf, and democracy allows us to choose someone different if we later change our mind. Democracy makes decision-makers accountable, putting us collectively back in control.

But democracy must evolve to meet the challenges of the Global Technological Revolution. This involves recognising that the model of democracy of the last 150 years, which successfully met the challenges of the Industrial Revolution, must evolve further. Our world is now more complex, more interconnected and more vulnerable than when democracy last evolved.

Some have long predicted that the Global Technological Revolution will enable the rich and powerful to avoid taxes, welfare payments and other responsibilities to fellow members of their community. More recently, with the rise of authoritarian populists, internet trolls and trade wars, others have painted a dystopian future where we are constantly monitored through digital devices, with our daily decisions controlled by anonymous algorithms, our environment destroyed, and where we are powerless against the whims of far-off bureaucrats, businesspeople and politicians.[1]

We can avoid this future, and instead take steps to ensure that the most effective tool for making decisions across large, diverse communities – democracy – is able to evolve effectively to meet new challenges. These include the challenge of beating global health pandemics, of regulating global technology so we can shape its future and not be in its thrall, of creating wealthier communities without destroying our environment, of providing better local public services even with less money, and of making international decisions fairly and in the interests of everyone, without letting an unaccountable elite make decisions that are only in their own interests.

This book suggests ways this might be done.

The rules of democracy

This book argues that democracy can evolve once more, as it has before. More accountable democracy, locally, nationally and internationally, would give us greater influence over decisions that impact on our communities, whether these are made by local nurses and social workers, national politicians or by Google or Facebook.

This updated model of democracy is not political, in the sense that it is neutral about the specific decisions that politicians take on our behalf. In democracies, we are each in control of who we elect to represent us politically when decisions are made – perhaps someone who wants to spend more on public health, or to spend less; or who supports migration, or who does not. That is our individual democratic choice. If a politician wants our vote, they must persuade us to give it to them. This book argues that, once we have elected a politician, we must hold them to account for the decisions that they take on our behalf.

We may disagree about who to vote for, but we surely agree that all politicians must compete fairly for our votes, and then play by the rules when they win. Ludwig Wittgenstein wrote in *Philosophical investigations* that language is as a game, where words have meaning in the context of the rules of a game played between speakers. If two speakers have a common understanding of the rules of the 'game' of language, they can then communicate by 'playing' by the same rules, sharing meanings through words. In a parallel way, this book describes the decision-making process of democracy in a way that the rules of a game might be described.

If I do not know the rules of football, I can be told that there are 11 people on each team, a goal of a certain size and a ball of certain dimensions. I can find out where to play the game, how long the game lasts and how the game is won. Players are allowed, for example, to kick the ball with their feet within certain lines, but they are not allowed to touch the ball with their hands or to pull their opponents' shirts. When we describe the rules in this way, we can learn to enjoy watching the game, or to play the game too, if we so wish.

The description of democracy in this book does not say who plays the game well. If we like football, we know that Brazil and Italy have strong footballing histories and many excellent players. We may nonetheless support our favourite local team. We debate past victories and recent losses, and how our team can increase its chances of success. But we do not much debate the rules of the game itself, unless we think our opponent has cheated.

It is the same with democracy. We may have our own team, whether Democrat or Republican (US), Labour or Conservative (UK). Which team (or political party) we choose to represent us when decisions are made is up to us. We want our team to win, and we discuss which players (that is, politicians) play well. We celebrate victories and regret losses, and we may give team managers (that is, political leaders) our advice on how our team can improve. But, as with football, we debate far less the rules of the game of democracy itself, except when we fear our political opponents may be cheating to win power.

This book describes the rules of the game of democracy, and how the rules might evolve – after all, the game of democracy is played for our benefit. The point of the game, rather than to score goals, is to make decisions on behalf of our community. Millions of us in our communities select the players by voting. Our player is our elected representative – maybe a Member of Parliament (MP), or a US senator, or a local councillor. They participate in the game of making decisions on our behalf. We can watch the game, if we want. We may watch a lot and follow politics obsessively. Or we may not be interested in watching much at all, in which case we may simply vote every few years, and then get on with the rest of our life.

But whatever our level of interest in politics, and whichever team we support, we should want the players to play by the rules of the game. If our team loses fairly, because more people vote for the other side, we may find an election result hard to take. But if we believe that the election was fair, we cannot dispute the result itself. If, however, we think that our team lost due to cheating or behaviour that was against the rules, then we might get angry, and rightly so. We may want the match to be played again and have a new election, or for those who cheated to be punished. We may even lose trust in democracy itself.[2]

In other words, just as with Wittgenstein's language game, we need shared, agreed rules by which to play the game of democracy. In practice, this also means having fair, independent referees to make sure that all those involved in the game stick to the rules, and to sanction any players who try to cheat.

When we watch sport, we do not go to see the referee. Indeed, we may be oblivious to the referee altogether. But there are moments in any game when the referee must decide whether a particular action is or is not within the rules. Was the ball in or out? Was there a foul or not? Did the ball cross the line? The referee does not make up the rules of the game, but must apply the rules fairly and consistently to both teams, without fear or favour.

Democracy, like a game, must be refereed to make sure it is fair. Our elected representatives – politicians – are the players in the game. The referees of democracy are judges and regulators. It is their responsibility to make sure that politicians play fairly, and stick to the rules.

For many years I was such a referee of democracy. From 2014 to 2020, I ran the UK's Independent Parliamentary Standards Authority, the watchdog responsible for regulating and paying taxpayers' money to 650 MPs, including for their salaries, pensions and expenses. For eight years before that, I was director at the National Audit Office and the Audit Commission, responsible for refereeing the use of public money spent by national and local government. In addition, for three years I was an adviser to the Centre for Public Scrutiny and for two years a consultant to the Prime Minister's Delivery Unit in Downing Street. In all these roles, I helped to ensure that politicians and public servants played by the rules. And they almost always did. Sometimes they did not. I wrote and published reports on those who wasted public money, with civil servants called to explain their actions before Parliament's Public Accounts Committee. I also made sure that politicians did not spend public money illegally. In a very few cases, I reported them to the police for suspected fraud. During my tenure, only one MP, Chris Davies, was convicted of submitting false expenses, leading those in his constituency to vote him out of Parliament.

I draw on this experience to describe the rules of democracy as the 'game' is currently played, focusing particularly on the Westminster-style parliamentary democracy that we have in the UK. I argue that the rules can evolve, so that, in the light of the current challenges to democracy, politicians and public services can play more fairly by better rules and be held to account by independent referees. In this way, we can improve democracy as a whole – not just how politicians act as our representatives, but how we participate in democracy too.

Rules in communities

Communities have always made rules to order the actions and behaviour of those who live in them. Over 4,000 years ago, King Hammurabi of Babylon placed stones around his kingdom that were inscribed with rules on what was and was not allowed. Rules, which we usually call laws and regulations, have existed ever since. The rules change as the needs of the community evolve.

In democracies, rules are set by elected representatives on our behalf. New laws are proposed and debated. Some are agreed and come into force in an attempt to create better rules that enhance the overall wellbeing of a community. These agreed rules, codified into enforceable law, form the basis of all well-ordered societies. Judges and others ensure that we obey these laws. And, in most democracies, judges are independent of politicians, so we can have confidence that, if we go to court, our case will be considered fairly.[3]

The laws of a community define the boundaries of acceptable behaviour, just as rules define how to play a game such as football, and also set its boundaries. The law also defines what will happen if we step beyond the boundaries of play. In football, we may be sent off the pitch. In a community, we may be sent to prison. The boundaries are determined by politicians, on our behalf. Judges, supported by the police and prosecutors, decide when the boundary has been breached and what sanction to impose.

The rules of the law give communities stability. Rightly, laws usually change slowly, which allows any new rules to be thoroughly debated before they are enforced on everyone. But communities also need more dynamic and flexible ways to ensure that their members obey the rules. This is so that we can go about our daily lives, guided by accepted norms and shared standards of behaviour, without needing new laws for an infinity of possible circumstances and ever-changing situations.

This is where regulation supports the law. The law creates a boundary that defines within a community what is allowable and what is not. Regulation informs how the law will be applied in detail, and allows for judgments to be made in individual cases within the boundary of the law. Thus, a national law might promote recycling or ban smoking, while regulation allows government agencies and local councils to decide how to inform people of the law, how to enforce it and what to do in individual circumstances when people break it. Regulation can respond more quickly to changing needs. And regulation can encourage compliance with the rules through incentives as well as through the sanction of the law.[4]

All systems need flexible, dynamic mechanisms to regulate them so that they do not fail. Our body will fail if it gets too hot or too cold. That is its law. But it regulates itself, too, so that we can survive constant changes in air temperature. Our blood retreats to our vital organs in the cold; we sweat in the heat. The animal world regulates itself, too, including through a hierarchy of predators that controls population growth. Locusts are eaten by lizards, who are eaten by snakes, who are eaten by owls.

Regulation can balance competing demands on a system in real time, and within fixed rules, so that a wider goal can be achieved. That goal may be the survival of our body, or the survival of our community. Democracy, like any other system, must be regulated too.

Regulating communities

Most activity in communities is already regulated. In the UK, the Food Standards Agency is responsible for food hygiene and applying standards of safe food preparation. The Civil Aviation

Authority issues pilot licences, inspects equipment at airports, sets security standards and protects travellers if an airline fails. The Health and Safety Executive enforces standards of workplace safety and investigates industrial accidents. And new vaccines, including those to combat COVID-19, are approved for use by regulators such as the Food and Drug Administration in the US and the Medicines and Healthcare products Regulatory Agency in the UK.

Regulators are the referees of the law. They ensure compliance with standards, as well as with the law itself. They may set prices or fees for those providing services to a community. They publish guidance, and act where laws are at risk of being broken. They can impose penalties, including fining or taking licences from nurses, teachers or pilots if there are concerns about their ability or behaviour. They may have the power of surveillance. They audit and inspect services, and publish findings and recommendations.

Where there are no referees in our communities, people must do the right thing without being told. This is self-regulation. Anyone who tries to stop smoking or lose weight without help knows that self-regulation can be hard. Some can do it, but others find it difficult to resist temptation. Little or no regulation is good in areas that are well understood and behaviour is generally good. Most driving is lightly regulated: we don't need traffic police at every street corner. Stronger regulation is necessary where risks are high, such as for approving new medicines. Weak regulation can lead to dangerous toys being sold to children, unsafe food being cooked in restaurants, and thieves setting up as insurance brokers.

Without rules and their referees, people are not held to account for failure or for cheating. Playing football without a referee may be fine for a kick-about in the park with friends, if our friends play fair. But a game without a referee is a bad idea when the stakes are higher.

Regulators should not be overzealous, creating hundreds of petty rules. Too much regulation is costly and counter-productive. In July 2017, enforcement officers from Tower Hamlets Council in London imposed a £150 fine on a five-year-old's kerbside lemonade stall as it contravened local regulations.[5] High costs of regulation encourage people to avoid rules instead of complying with them, and can inhibit investment in innovation and improvement. Regulation then becomes more trouble than it is worth, like a referee constantly stopping the game, or sending half the team off the pitch. It makes the whole game less enjoyable, and it is unfair on those who choose to play by the rules.

Regulators must get the balance right between too much and too little regulation, checking demands for greater freedom against the need for more protection. Good regulators get the balance right: stopping abuse, protecting the weak, encouraging improvement and letting the players play the game.

Good regulators, like good referees, go unnoticed. Only in moments of dispute or controversy do we spot them. They blow their whistle, stop the game and take action. If their decision is fair, then both teams accept it, albeit grudgingly, and then play on.

Referees are never loved, but their role is essential for games to avoid acrimony and conflict. Good regulation helps communities work well, creating stability and predictability as we go about our daily lives. Rules are applied in ways that we can broadly trust to be firm but not oppressive, and always independent, consistent and fair.

Regulating democracy

Just as unregulated wine merchants might be tempted to add water to their bottles, or unregulated auditors might ignore irregular payments in company accounts, so unregulated politicians may be tempted to behave badly too. The job of politicians, in part, is to persuade us to believe in them and to vote for them so they can gain power. Most do so with skill, dedication and integrity. But a few are, regrettably, tempted to cheat, steal, break the law, tell lies, break promises or sacrifice others to achieve influence.

That is why the game of democracy must have agreed rules that are enforced by independent referees such as judges and regulators. This ensures that politicians behave well, and that all parts of the democratic system work effectively on our collective behalf.

Politicians are, of course, already subject to the law, and some have been punished for breaking it. In the UK, Jeffrey Archer MP was imprisoned for perjury in 1987, MPs Elliot Morley and David Chaytor went to jail for expenses fraud in 2011, and in 2019, Fiona Onasanya MP was found guilty of lying to the police to avoid a speeding fine. A few senators in the US, and parliamentarians in Japan, Australia, Italy, Spain and elsewhere, have all been convicted of crimes including fraud, lewd behaviour and giving false statements.[6]

But in an important way, democracy is unlike other areas of life that are regulated. Democracy is a game of decision-making. In this game, we choose politicians to decide, on our behalf, which rules we want our community to play by. Politicians play the game by debating and gathering support for one idea or another, until there is a majority in favour of setting a new rule or changing an existing one. Once they have agreed to a changed rule (and perhaps passed a law), they move on to debate other possible rule changes.

Agreeing how to change the rules for a community is usually contentious. There are often good arguments both for and against a particular change. In virtually all areas of their work, politicians are debating changes to rules as they will impact on others, whether farmers, dentists, children, people with disabilities or exporters. In contrast, when debating whether to change the rules of democracy itself, politicians are debating the rules of their own game and how changed rules may impact on them in a very personal way. Decision-making and rule-setting are the whole point of the game of democracy. This makes it hard to ask politicians, the players of the game, to set the rules of their own game while they are actually in the process of playing it. It is like asking footballers to agree the dimensions of the goal while either defending it or kicking the ball towards it.

This is not to say that democracy has no rules; it does. These are outlined in the next chapter. To enforce the rules, democracy has referees, too, including Boundary Commissions and Electoral Commissions, to ensure that the way we elect politicians to represent us is conducted independently and fairly. These referees of democracy have been called an 'integrity branch' of constitutional governance that limits 'the predictable efforts by reigning politicians to entrench themselves against popular reversals at the polls'.[7]

But the rules of democracy can be made more effective to increase our confidence that politicians are playing by the rules. This is because our current rules were set before the changes brought about by a Global Technological Revolution and a global health pandemic. Our world is very different to the one it was 30 years ago. The old rules of democracy are no longer good enough, and need to evolve.

Better, updated rules of democracy will make it easier for us to discuss and agree potential solutions to intractable or global problems, whether pandemics, inequalities, online abuse, refugee crises or climate change. And better rules of democracy will help to ensure that everyone affected by decisions is more fairly represented at the decision–making table. This does not happen well enough now. This book puts forward suggestions for improvements.

1

The importance of democracy

Communities differ in many ways, including in the rules they set for their decision-making. Core 'rules' for decision-making in democracies have nonetheless evolved over time, as follows:

1. People are born with equal rights, including to freedom and safety from harm.
2. People naturally form communities of various sizes, including families, tribes, towns and nations. These communities provide the people who are in them with benefits, including security, identity and health.
3. People are required to cede some of their rights, such as to unfettered freedom, to their communities, in return for benefits, such as security.
4. These benefits cost the communities money and effort to provide. Communities raise the money to provide the benefits, mostly by imposing taxes on the people of their own community.
5. People in each community must decide which benefits their community should provide to its members, as well as how money should be raised to fund these benefits. Rather than allow an absolute ruler or small elite to make these decisions in their narrow interests, people in democratic communities develop ways to choose representatives to make decisions on behalf of the community as a whole. These representatives are the politicians elected in democracies.
6. The decisions themselves become codified into rules, such as laws and accepted practice. People in communities are required to adhere to these rules on penalty of enforceable

sanctions. The laws and accepted practice change over time in line with the decisions made by elected representatives on behalf of the communities they represent.

7. Elected representatives establish institutions to provide the benefits to the community and to raise the money to fund them, in line with their decisions and the rules they have created. These institutions include public services and all other services funded through taxation.

Democracy has been described in many ways, and these sweeping statements cover much ground, but in these core 'rules' can be recognised a summary of modern representative democracy: where all adults have the right to vote periodically for others to represent their interests, and where these representatives form councils, assemblies, parliaments and senates to decide how to raise and spend taxes in the interests of the communities they represent, to codify their decisions into laws and regulations, and to create, change and abolish institutions to bring about the benefits desired.

The history of democracy, and its manifestations over time and across continents, is much studied. A comprehensive account is in John Keane's (2009) *The life and death of democracy*. Democracy itself started at least 2,400 years ago, as recorded in Plato's *Republic*. Many giants of philosophy and practice have helped democracy to evolve since then. Niccolò Machiavelli (1469–1527) and Alexis de Tocqueville (1805–59) described the systems of governance they witnessed in medieval Italy and the early United States, respectively. How best to create ordered governance in free societies much preoccupied Thomas Hobbes (1588–1679), John Locke (1632–1704), Edmund Burke (1729–97) and John Stuart Mill (1806–73), among many others. The arguments of Jean-Jacques Rousseau (1712–78), Thomas Paine (1737–1809), Mary Wollstonecraft (1759–97), Karl Marx (1818–83) and others helped to extend rights, including to working men and women. Those who championed democracy and hoped to improve it include John Dewey (1859–1952), Karl Popper (1902–94), Hannah Arendt (1906–75) and John Rawls (1921–2002). The works of US presidents Thomas Jefferson (1743–1826) and Abraham Lincoln (1809–65) indelibly shaped the democratic governance of their country. And the importance of institutions to democracy are central to the work of Max Weber (1864–1920) and Daron Acemoglu and James Robinson's excellent 2013 book *Why nations fail.*[1]

All these and many other thinkers helped democracy to evolve. And democracy has survived because it is an efficient way to resolve complex social challenges. Democracy allows those with a stake in an issue to have a say, so that decision-making can draw on the collective insight, intelligence and interests of the whole community.

Where a decision-making community is small, all its members can potentially input into each decision. Those in a shared apartment with friends, for example, can all meet each week to decide how to use common resources, such as the kitchen and bathroom, and how to cover communal costs.

As a community gets bigger, and its decisions get more complicated, we do not want to spend time debating and agreeing every detail about how our community works. In a community of 30 houses in a village or housing estate, one resident may liaise with the drainage company on behalf of everyone else, and another may ensure the shared road is well maintained. The other residents can get on with their lives with confidence that they can find out about and contribute to important decisions that affect them. The community balances a desire to participate in decision-making with the impracticality of asking everyone's opinion about everything.

On a larger scale, communities the size of towns or countries have learned similar lessons. Involving everyone in each decision is impossible in practice. The device of holding a referendum where millions of people vote on a specific question carries risk. The people of Ireland decided the specific issue of legalising abortion in a 2018 referendum, with the result accepted. But complex issues are hard to summarise in a simple question, creating opportunities for misleading advertising. In 2016 the people of the UK were asked in a referendum whether to stay in the European Union (EU). Those voting to 'leave' or to 'remain' accessed such different information about the decision that politicians spent the next three years debating what had been voted for and how to achieve it. The problems inherent in calling a referendum have led some countries to rerun a referendum to get a more convenient result. The people of Denmark approved the EU's Maastricht treaty in 1993 only after rejecting it in 1992. And in France, after a draft EU constitution was rejected by its people in 2007, national politicians decided not to risk a second referendum and approved changes in 2008 without asking voters again. For such reasons, and despite referendums being seen by some in the US as a useful tool that can increase public satisfaction with political debate,[2] the Netherlands decided in 2018 to ban national referendums, and the Swiss constitution requires two separate votes on fundamental or particularly contested issues.

Large democratic communities have therefore generally recognised that the election of representatives enables everyone to have a voice in decision-making, without needing to involve everyone in every decision. We choose someone to take decisions on our behalf, maybe because we like them and what they believe, or because they come from our own community, or because they have persuaded us that they have our interests at heart and will represent us fairly.

It is by electing people to represent us that we can, through them, debate the issues of the day and find ways to address social needs. Our representatives try to reflect the wishes of all those who elected them and make the difficult trade-offs between spending or saving money, between allocating money to education or defence or health or housing, and choosing between benefiting one group of people or another.

Our elected representatives – politicians – do a vital and important job. Their role is to represent thousands, tens of thousands, or hundreds of thousands of people, and try to weigh evidence and reconcile vastly different views. And while they try to reflect the needs of a community and respond to its conflicting demands, they must also try to lead the community and inform its members about impending change and its potential impact. This means that they must both lead a community and follow its lead. They must know when to cajole, when to take a stand, when to negotiate or compromise, and when to change their mind. This is a difficult balance. We need politicians who are good at their jobs, just as we need plumbers and doctors who are good at theirs. Indeed, leadership of democratic communities requires vastly superior skills than those required by an authoritarian leader who can simply say: 'Do as I tell you, or else.'

However bad their reputation, most politicians generally care deeply about representing their community well, and helping their constituents to become wealthier and healthier. Their job depends on it. In most cases, there is a defined physical area that a politician represents, whether it is a neighbourhood, a town, a province or a state. They generally get to know their area well, including its towns and streets, shops and businesses and, above all, its people. Even if they started as out-of-towners parachuted in by party bosses, most politicians work hard to serve their real, physical, geographical community as well as they can, and to be seen to be doing so.

The job of a politician, like all jobs, can be done badly. Indeed, it is a hard job to do well. The Global Technological Revolution has made it harder. The delicate balancing act of representing a spectrum of divergent views within a community, while also standing up for what they believe, is now done in the permanent glare of the internet and social media. Politicians are vilified for what they say, what they do and how they vote. Some have been killed for doing their jobs. In the UK, Jo Cox and David Amess were murdered as they met their constituents in 2016 and 2021 respectively; Steve Scalise was shot at a baseball game in the US in 2017; and Kosovo Serb Oliver Ivanovic was shot and killed in 2018. Elected leaders have been killed in Pakistan, Israel, Egypt, Haiti and Chile. The list is too long.

We may dislike our own politicians because they hold views that are unlike our own. Or because they change their mind. Or because some politicians really are idiotic, chaotic or dislikeable. But in a democracy, our politicians are there to represent our whole community, in all its diversity. It should be no surprise that they broadly (although not completely by sex or race) resemble the people they represent; we may also sometimes say things without thinking, or change our minds, or even be foolish at times. Our representatives represent us nonetheless. And whatever their beliefs or skills, almost all the

21,000 local and national politicians elected in the UK want to do that honourably and to make a positive difference to their communities.

Their job is to represent a range of views and debate issues on our behalf. We choose, through democracy, to give our representatives the difficult task of working out in detail how to improve public services by spending limited amounts of public money. Most of us would not want to do that job ourselves.

We can also remind ourselves that representative democracy has not come easily. It took many centuries for the right to choose decision-makers to be extended beyond rich men. In the UK, working men were not able to vote until 1867 and women not until 1928. Those struggles eventually led to the consensus described in core rules of democracy, where all adults have an equal right to vote, and where the flexibility and responsiveness of politicians is balanced by the stability and expertise of democratically established institutions. This intricate arrangement for making community decisions, of stable institutions and flexible politicians accountable to their communities, is a historical achievement that we should cherish.

Decision-making in democracies results from the constant interaction of billions of unique individuals, exchanging ideas in multiple communities, just as the global economy is the result of billions of individual financial transactions. In a democracy, we each use our judgement and draw on our history and culture, as well as on fact and reasoning, when choosing who we want to represent us. Our elected politicians then debate and decide actions on our behalf.

Democracy is humanity's most complex social innovation. It is the social equivalent of the human brain. Each idea exchanged, each conversation and debate and each vote is like an individual synapse firing in a brain, inconsequential on its own, but collectively, across a trillion synapses, or a billion conversations, of unmappable complexity. By granting equal rights to every adult person, and in creating mechanisms for making complex decisions and taking action in a structured and managed way, democracy is the collective brain of our community. Like damaged brains, however, a democracy that does not take account of its members will make imperfect decisions. But if we each participate in democracy, and if our elected representatives play their difficult role well, democracy gives communities the potential to find ways to deal peacefully with change and disagreement.

Democracy over authoritarianism

Many people, both historically and now, have nonetheless been sceptical of democracy and its value. Some say that their own politicians do not listen to their concerns or cannot influence decisions. As a result, they may feel powerless or frustrated. Some may even think politicians exploitative or corrupt, and become angry.

Such feelings of powerlessness, frustration and anger can lead to campaigns and demonstrations, marches and boycotts. They can also lead to a loss of faith in democracy as a mechanism to address social change and resolve social problems, and a belief that we just need someone strong to lead a community through destabilising times.

Strong authoritarian leaders can be attractive at times of significant social change, like a Moses leading people to safety from the wilderness. They can give a much-needed sense of certainty to communities feeling dislocated, whether they are trying to preserve things as they were or to make things better. Hannah Arendt, in *The origins of totalitarianism* (1951), among others, has written powerfully about the attraction of such leaders.

Authoritarian rulers have a sad history, encompassing, just in the 20th century, military governments in South America, Africa and Asia, one-party rule in the Soviet Union and China, and murderous dictators in Italy and Germany. The destabilisation caused by the Global Technological Revolution has made strong rulers appealing again. In 2018, 18 per cent of people in the US thought that military rule would be a good idea and 24 per cent wanted a strong leader who could ignore interference from democracy and the courts. In the UK in 2019, while its Parliament was in deadlock over how to leave the EU, fully 54 per cent of people said they needed a strong leader who was willing to break rules if necessary. Authoritarian and populist leaders have been elected across Europe and the Americas, as well as again in Italy and Germany. The international think tank Freedom House reported in 2021 that 75 per cent of the world's population lived in a country where democracy had been eroded in the previous year.[3]

By their very nature, authoritarian leaders do not play by the rules of democracy that involve consulting others and reaching consensus with their community before making decisions. Instead, they tend to take decisions alone or within small cliques. They favour one part of their community over others and ignore contrary views. They impose constraints on any who do not share their views. The favoured groups benefit from protection and access to economic and other opportunities. The penalised groups, whether defined by politics, place of origin, ethnicity or religion, have less access to education, housing or employment, and may be subject to threats, expulsion or violence.

Authoritarian leaders usually claim that decisive action is necessary to bring order and calm to communities divided by social change or at risk of external threats. And, because they dislike the debate and compromise that are required when playing by the rules of democracy, authoritarian leaders tend to impose their own solutions to social problems, regardless of opposition or evidence.

Authoritarian leaders do not want referees of democracy to hold them to account for playing by the rules. Even in democracies, authoritarian politicians try to ignore the rules and pressurise the referees and regulators. In undemocratic communities, authoritarian leaders simply set their own rules and play without a referee. They are the team captain, and they want to win. So they pay off the referee, and may even get rid of the opposing team altogether.

Playing a game without agreed, enforceable rules may be fun for the biggest bully in the playground. But, even aside from the moral arguments against authoritarian leaders and their impact, this way of playing the game of decision-making, rather than through an open democracy where all members of communities are fairly represented with equal rights, creates three risks to authoritarians: that their decisions are illegal, arbitrary and ineffective.

Authoritarian leaders may play the game by their own rules in their own domain with impunity, for a while. But they are usually breaking rules elsewhere, and may eventually be held to account. Authoritarian leaders age. Laws change. If the authoritarian leader loses power, and they have caused suffering, they can be brought to justice. This has happened in Argentina, the Balkans, Chad, Chile, Egypt, the Gambia, Guatemala, Indonesia, Senegal, Spain, Ukraine and elsewhere. International law can prosecute human rights abuses and instances of genocide. Since 2002, the International Criminal Court has investigated or prosecuted crimes of genocide, including in 11 countries, from Burundi to Uganda, and publicly indicted 44 individuals. Although justice is always slow, if they ignore all the rules, authoritarian leaders still risk being punished later by those who have chosen more fairly to play by agreed rules, and who appeal to the referee for justice.

Authoritarian approaches to decision-making, which fail to take account of the interests of all members of a community, also risk being more arbitrary and less effective over the long term. In controlled experiments, large groups tend to make better decisions than smaller ones.[4] It is unlikely that the expertise and creativity needed to address major social change in a community can be found in a small subset of its membership. Authoritarian leaders may think they have all the answers. And some pretend that social change has not happened at all if it threatens their power and influence. In China in 1371, in Japan in 1641 and in Bhutan until 1999, authoritarian leaders put up physical and legal walls to prevent the fundamental social changes that would result from trade with foreigners. Other authoritarian actions, including the imprisonment, expulsion or death of opponents, attempt to limit the influence of those who are bringing change.

The short-term impact of these actions may be to preserve the status quo, but the fundamental forces of social change rarely disappear. The self-isolation of China and Japan centuries ago did not stop European trade. Instead, authoritarian rulers damaged their own communities. They reduced the skills and experience of the very people in their own community who could find ways to respond to social change. And they excluded many talented and thoughtful people from contributing to important decision-making processes altogether.

Faced with discrimination, many marginalised groups simply leave, and take their money, skills and dynamism elsewhere. This happened to the Moors expelled from Spain in 1492, the Huguenot Protestants who fled France from 1685 when Louis XIV deprived them of their religious and civil liberties, and the millions who escaped Nazi Germany and the communist Soviet Union in the 20th century. This action takes financial and human resources out of the authoritarian community and gives them freely to more welcoming communities who can use the money, skills and dynamism to their advantage, as the US and the UK did successfully during and after the Second World War. The International Monetary Fund (IMF) found in 2016 that immigrants' skills and ideas had boosted living standards in the US and UK by 30 per cent. The World Bank found in 2000 that African countries developed faster economically when they were democracies than when they were not, as individuals gain freedom to discover not only what makes them happy and successful, but also what can bring success and wealth to their whole community. An analysis of data between 1960 and 2019 from multiple sources found that democracies convincingly slowed the spread of pandemics too.[5]

In these and other ways, authoritarian leaders damage their own communities. Like an ostrich, they stick their head in the ground and hope that change will go away. Major technological and social change rarely does. Printing did not disappear after 1440. The Industrial Revolution did not stop after 1820. Now, too, the Global Technological Revolution is here for good.

Choosing an authoritarian leader as a response to fear and change is akin to slamming the door and curling up in bed following a major setback in life, such as a divorce, redundancy or bereavement. It is a natural reaction of bewilderment and pain, and of a need to retreat in the face of deep disappointment or confusion. Yet, in due course, even after a major change, most of us try to regroup and focus on the future, and once again open the door to re-engage with the changed world outside.

The apparent strength of authoritarian leaders is rigidity, which, like concrete, may crack under pressure. The true strength of democracy comes from stable institutions made flexible, like wood, by being accountable to representatives elected regularly by the communities they serve.

2

The evolution of democracy

Democracy is an exceptionally good way of making complex, broadly consensual decisions within large communities. But the current rules of democracy are no longer sufficient. This is because the Global Technological Revolution has led to a speed and depth of change unseen since the Industrial Revolution 200 years ago. Of many familiar examples of this transformative change, here are three, from transportation, travel and telephony.

The international transportation of almost all goods until the 1970s was by packing them loose into cargo ships. Today, container ships each carry 1,500 standard six-metre metal boxes. Over 1.8 billion metric tons of goods were carried in containers in 2017, ten times more than in 1980. Of the cost of a US$5 T-shirt manufactured in Asia and sold in Europe, the cost of transportation is only 2 cents. By 2015, 48 per cent of the UK's food supply came from overseas, with the annual value of overall imports more than doubling in 30 years to £600 billion by 2019.

Our travel patterns have changed similarly. In 1980, UK residents went abroad 17 million times, and spent £3 billion. By 2017, this had increased to 73 million visits abroad, with spending of £45 billion. Across the world, pre-pandemic, there were 1.2 billion tourist arrivals every year. And at any one time, until COVID-19 cleared the skies, there were almost 10,000 planes in the air, carrying 1.2 million people between countries at more than 500 miles per hour.

In terms of telephony, the cost in 1980 of a three-minute transatlantic phone call of often poor quality was US$12.60, the equivalent of about US$38.50 today. The internet has now made international communication, whether via WhatsApp,

FaceTime or Skype, essentially free for everyone who has internet access.

This increased global connectivity has brought massive benefits to communities in every part of the planet. Goods are cheaper and more varied. Children and adults, wherever they live, can access learning from the world's brightest minds. Those in minority groups can find friends and support online. And families can stay in touch in a way that was unimaginable a few decades ago. There are many more economic, educational and social benefits besides.

In addition to its benefits, however, the Global Technological Revolution has also brought major social changes that have implications for democracy.

Physical boundaries are now less important. By bringing together buyers and sellers across continents, and international friends and relatives, the Global Technological Revolution has expanded our horizons so far that the horizons themselves may seem irrelevant. In some aspects of our life, it makes no difference where we live. As long as we can access the internet, we can buy almost any product we want, right now. It is then shipped instantly to wherever we happen to be. While we make this purchase, we could be watching one of a million videos uploaded minutes ago thousands of miles away. And we can work in Mexico for a Taiwanese company that sells to customers in Ethiopia. We all spend part of our life online. We connect with work online, we chat online about sport or politics, we find lovers and meet friends too. We think this commonplace. It is, now.

Yet, despite our extensive online lives, as a flesh-and-blood person, we are each still a physical and not a digital object. Even with access to the whole world through an internet that has no visible geography, we live physically in a real home in a real street in a specific local community. Whatever exciting stuff is happening online, at some point we need to open our front door and put out the rubbish, take our children to school, visit the doctor, and travel on roads to visit friends and family, as well as protect ourselves against a virus that is real, not digital. This means that we still need flesh-and-blood public services to work well when we need them, wherever we live in real life.

In democracies, we make sure our public services work by electing people to make decisions that will make the services better. This representative democracy has worked well enough in many places in the past, but the Global Technological Revolution is posing challenges that democracy does not currently have the capability to respond to.

First, the current challenge is different to those challenges of the past because it is global. We lack effective mechanisms to hold multinational companies to account, or to stop criminals from acting beyond the law by moving money around the world, or to enforce action on global environmental issues including climate change. National politicians can debate these issues, and even agree laws to prohibit certain activities, but new laws in Switzerland or South Africa to ban online abuse will not stop it from happening to residents of Basel or Bloemfontein, let alone elsewhere. Attempts to regulate tech firms are met with threats, such as Google's threat in January 2021 to withdraw its search engine from Australia. Global agreements on climate change do not prompt the necessary action by governments and businesses.

Second, the Global Technological Revolution has destroyed professions and communities as well as created new ones. Following the Industrial Revolution, the farriers who shoed horses, and the coopers who made barrels, and thousands of others who worked on the land, lost their livelihoods. Two hundred years on, the current economic and social changes are impacting not only manual workers in factories and warehouses, but increasingly professionals, as machines take their jobs, whether they are translators, telephonists, bookkeepers or bank cashiers. Algorithms, robots and artificial intelligence are reducing the need for human expertise. Some communities are struggling with the consequences of economic decline and emigration, losing shops, businesses and their young people to cities or countries abroad. These communities feel left behind at the same time as other communities are struggling to cope with the new arrivals, particularly if the incomers have a different skin colour or religion, or need financial support, housing and access to public services as they settle into a new life.[1]

Third, a new division has emerged between those who have benefited more from the Global Technological Revolution, who may be more educated, more urban and more international in outlook, and those who have benefited less, who may be more rooted in their local community and its traditions, and perhaps work in traditional industries. David Goodhart, in his 2017 book *The road to somewhere*, memorably described this as a division between 'Anywheres', who are urban, mobile, wealthy and educated, and 'Somewheres', who are older, poorer, less educated and stay close to home. Many countries are internally divided in this way. In some places, old political parties have split and new ones have formed as a partial response to this change. In others, people have elected populists who deny the facts of globalisation and promise to recapture a golden past without immigration, and with all the old jobs back.

The internet and social media have amplified such divisions. Debates about issues now take place permanently online. Comments are dominated by those with extreme views rather than those prepared to listen to others' opinions. This allows less space for the necessary compromises and trade-offs of decision-making in democracies. Those who dislike a decision made by politicians feel cheated and fight on, contacting thousands of 'friends' in the echo chamber of social media who think the same as them. This risks disenchantment with democracy itself if those who dislike a decision made democratically refuse to accept that the decision was reached fairly and according to agreed rules.

Fourth, the internet and social media are also being exploited by some politicians. They can spread half-true or completely untrue assertions faster and more widely than ever before. Some are elected on the basis of outright lies or comments that are impossible to disprove. Politicians who are grossly disrespectful of their voters, and who get away with telling lies for personal gain, may also lead some to question the effectiveness of the rules of democracy.

In addition, the anonymity of the internet and social media, and the willingness of big tech firms to take adverts from anyone who pays, has led to coordinated campaigns to undermine democratic processes. Russia paid for social media adverts to target voters in the US during the 2016 presidential election, campaigners in the UK used fake social media accounts to avoid spending rules and persuade voters to leave the EU, and WhatsApp was awash with fake news during the general election in India in 2019.[2] If we think that an election in our community is being influenced unfairly, we are right to worry that democracy is not as strong as it should be.

And finally, the anonymity of the internet and social media is also being used to bully and abuse politicians, 24/7. Death threats are common, and many politicians fear they are being stalked. Some have been attacked, and a few killed. Even those not getting abuse are burdened by thousands of emails, posts and tweets a day from people in their community, all expecting an instant reply. In response, some politicians distance themselves from their own community out of fear, or choose to leave politics altogether.[3] This risks leaving decision-making about our communities in the hands only of those politicians who can tolerate abuse or who are bullies themselves. A truly representative range of people will no longer want to become politicians. This weakens the effectiveness of democratic decision-making for all of us.

These factors collectively damage our faith in democracy, and suggest that the current rules of democracy are not working well enough.

The Accountability Gap

The rules of democracy must evolve to close two gaps created by the Global Technological Revolution. The first is a gap in accountability.

Whether we are concerned about global warming, immigration, technology, capitalism or COVID-19, we may share a perception that others, whether businesspeople, bureaucrats or politicians, are making decisions about our lives, our communities and our planet over which we have no control. It is an uncomfortable feeling. In the workplace, feeling a lack of control leads directly to increased stress and lower productivity.[4]

As a result, some have argued that we should 'take back control'. This is not just a Brexit slogan – the same sentiments are evident in independence movements in Scotland and Catalonia. Nor is it just in the US that the loss of economic control led to calls by Donald Trump's presidential campaign and others to put 'America first'. Ghana has lost 80 per cent of its textile jobs and Kenya half its clothing industry due to imports from overseas. Immigration has exacerbated these fears, especially when money is tight, and jobs and housing are scarce.

There is also widespread anger at the destruction of the natural environment, with concerns that there are too few controls over climate change, pollution or overfishing, and that global oil and mining companies can do as they please. There is parallel anger at the unrestrained power of large technological firms that successfully avoid paying taxes. According to a 2016 ruling from the EU, for example, Apple paid just 0.005 per cent in tax on its profits in Ireland in 2014. Tech firms also do little to protect the vulnerable against online abuse, illegal or distressing internet content or cyber-attack. In March 2019, the murder of 50 people in New Zealand mosques was live-streamed on YouTube and uploaded 1.5 million times on Facebook. Neither governments nor victims feel they have any control.

Reckless bankers are rarely held to account either. The banking crisis of 2008 led to a loss of trust in financial services and broader anger with the rich, with marches in Wall Street, the City of London, Frankfurt and elsewhere. Banks were rescued with £850 billion of public money in the UK and an initial US$700 billion in the US. Yet bankers' personal bonuses continued, showing no decline between the peak of the financial boom in 2007 and 2011. The losers were the 2 million people in the US alone who lost their jobs as unemployment climbed from 4.7 per cent in late 2007 to 7.4 per cent by December 2008.[5] Other losers included anyone who depended on public services in the decade of austerity and the reduced public spending that followed.

Globalisation and technology have also given the upper hand to international criminals who launder over US$1,000 billion a year across borders through casinos, precious metals and cash. Now they can evade the law through 1,800 global electronic crypto-currencies, such as Bitcoin or Ethereum, where money laundering is easier than through regulated banks. Crypto transactions are fast, anonymous, irreversible and untraceable. And criminals extort payments of US$5 billion a year through software 'ransom attacks'. It is very difficult to bring them to justice.[6]

In each of these areas, there is inadequate accountability. This applies to polluters, tech giants, big pharma, bankers and international criminals, or even just regular companies that move jobs abroad. Globalisation and new technologies have enabled them to prosper. But it can feel impossible to challenge their policies or decisions, or even to know who can do so on our behalf. Stories such as that of Thomas Reid, the Irish farmer who held out against the financial and political might of the tech giant Intel, are celebrated because they are so unusual.[7]

The concept of accountability includes notions of fairness, honesty, responsiveness, responsibility and integrity, and is closely linked with ideas of effective democracy. Being accountable means complying (or being made to comply) with the rules. If someone is accountable, they must behave correctly and do things in the right way, or risk being punished, whether by being sacked or being taken to court. It means playing by the rules.[8]

Where there is accountability, we can trust that someone will take responsibility, including for financial or environmental damage. Accountability gives people incentives to act in the interests of others, and not just themselves, because they know that there will be consequences if they do not. Accountable organisations have more legitimacy, whether they are businesses that are answerable to their customers or public services to their users. Without accountability, there is nobody to challenge when things go wrong, and we find it hard to get redress or justice. And in a democracy, where there is accountability, politicians like US President Harry Truman, who had a sign in his office saying 'The Buck Stops Here', know that they are answerable to their voters, and that we can kick them out of office when things go wrong and replace them with others. Such should be the consequences of not playing by the rules.

The Expectation Gap

In addition to an Accountability Gap, a second social impact of the Global Technological Revolution has been as disruptive. This is the dissatisfaction caused by our increased expectations of goods and services, including those services funded from public money. This has created an Expectation Gap.

The internet has created a new shop front for global brands, with massive financial opportunities to firms prepared, as Mark Zuckerberg was at Facebook, to 'move fast and break things'. Amazon started by selling books. It now sells everything, and it takes up to 60 per cent of every sale. eBay links buyers and sellers across the world and takes a 10 per cent cut. Firms like Deliveroo, which operates in 800 towns and cities, and Uber, which is in 10,000 towns and cities, carry food and people from A to B at the touch of a screen. All this and more are now totally familiar. But it represents a commercial revolution, and a social revolution in the way we buy things.

Online firms have grown so fast because we value their services, and we like the instant gratification they give. If we want something new, we can buy it right now, from the phone in our hand. Amazon can deliver it in two hours. If we cannot wait to see a film at a cinema, we can download it and watch it now, on Netflix. If we are hungry, we can get sushi, pizza or fresh vegetables brought to our door within minutes. And if we are not happy with the service we receive, we can switch to another company immediately. The internet has enabled us to gratify our desires instantly, whether we desire clothes, food, entertainment, friendship or sex. We now consider this kind of instant gratification to be normal and legitimate. Waiting is for fools.

But it is not just instant delivery that we expect. The internet has raised our expectations higher. Not only do we want the stuff we bought before, but faster. We want new stuff too. Social media allows us to observe the intimate lives of the most privileged people on the planet. It's fascinating. But it causes dissatisfaction too. We see people online who have lots and lots of things that we do not. We used to see wealth only in glossy magazines or on TV; now the wealthy are permanently in our sight.

By vastly increasing our knowledge of what we *could* have, the internet has also massively raised our expectations of what we *should* have. And it has raised our expectations of public services too.

We expect commercial services online to be fast, good and cheap, like Amazon, Apple or Uber, all recent creations. They are becoming our benchmark. But when we expect something similar from public services, we generally receive health, education and housing that were designed to meet the needs of our grandparents.

In the UK, we do not want to wait an average of 28 minutes for an ambulance, as we had to in December 2019, before COVID-19, or 47 minutes for someone to pick up the phone at the tax office of HMRC (Her Majesty's Revenue and Customs), as in October 2015, or two weeks for an appointment with a local doctor, as in August 2019, also before COVID-19. Nor do we expect combustible cladding on our home, as was the case for 470 social housing apartment buildings across the UK when one of them, Grenfell Tower, caught fire in June 2017, resulting in the death of 72 of its residents.[9] When accessing public services, we cannot generally go to a competitor. We must accept the schools, clinics, roads and air quality we are given. But we may expect better nonetheless.

The gap between what we expect from public services and what they provide is getting bigger. Those who remember a time before the Global Technological Revolution may be prepared to accept slow, poor-quality public services as the most that can reasonably be expected. But we are likely to put up with inadequate public services less and less as time goes by, especially as we become accustomed to fast, high-quality services online. We may also become more reluctant to pay taxes for slow, poor-quality public services. We expect more for our money.

The widening Expectation Gap between what we want from public services and what we get can lead to dissatisfaction with the way public services are run in general. In the UK, 29 per cent of people said in 2017 that they were not happy with the National Health Service (NHS), and 21 per cent said in 2018 that were unhappy with the railways.[10] This is hardly a sign of service failure, but both scores were the worst in a decade.

This Expectation Gap is a further challenge to the effectiveness of the existing rules of democracy as a mechanism of bringing benefits to our communities.

Democracy has evolved before

Democracy can respond and evolve in the face of these challenges. The Industrial Revolution 200 years ago presented similar challenges – democracy responded and evolved.

In pre-industrial times, there were few public services. The wealthy paid for private doctors and private tutors. Some landowners provided housing, basic education and healthcare for those working their land. And some religious bodies supported the homeless, the sick and the destitute. But mostly, people had to fend for themselves.

That changed with the Industrial Revolution.[11] Factories attracted hundreds of thousands of rural peasants to towns and cities. Birmingham and Liverpool more than quadrupled in size, from 70,000 residents each in 1800 to 300,000 and 380,000 people respectively in 1850. In the same period, the population of London increased from 950,000 to 2.5 million. Cities couldn't cope. There was squalid housing, homelessness and destitution, unsanitary streets with open sewers, rampant disease and high infant mortality, and widespread poverty and crime.

Industrialisation brought many benefits, as globalisation and technology have today, but there were enormous social costs too, particularly after cholera struck London in 1831 and again in 1847, killing over 100,000 people. The wealthy and the new middle classes came to realise that these social problems had to be addressed. They were reported on daily in the 1,000 newspapers that sprang up across the country, and written about movingly in contemporary novels, including by Charles Dickens. In other words, expectations increased among people in 19th-century Britain about the public services that they should be able to access in their newly industrial society. This parallels the Expectation Gap that has arisen today.

The Parliament of the 19th century responded to the higher expectations. In 1833, children under the age of 9 were required, for the first time, to spend two hours every day in school, and in 1842 it became illegal for children under 10 to work in mines below ground. Vaccination became freely available in 1840 and made compulsory in 1853. In 1844, a Royal Commission was established to examine how to improve health in towns and cities. And after much debate, an income tax was permanently established in 1842. Public spending increased from £14 million a year in 1850 to £70 million in 1860. The money was used to meet people's increased expectations and to address social need, particularly in cities. In London, the first police force was created in 1829, an underground railway in 1863 and a city-wide sewerage system in 1865. Once these public services were created, communities came routinely to expect better safety, efficient transportation and decent sewerage as their normal and legitimate entitlements in return for their taxes.

These changes took place because of decisions made by democratic politicians acting to respond to the needs of their communities. None of these changes was easy. Each was fought over. Those who feared that they would lose power or influence were reluctant to allow change, and sometimes only did so under duress. Those who wanted a say over decisions about their lives and their communities, including the new middle classes and the urban poor, fought equally hard to gain equality and access to influence.

For these changes to take place at all, the rules of democracy had to evolve.

In 1820, cities such as Birmingham, with its population of 85,000, and Leeds, with its 70,000 inhabitants, had no elected representatives at all in the UK Parliament, while some small communities, including the 42 residents of Grampound in Cornwall, the 32 voters of Dunwich in Suffolk and the 7 voters of Old Sarum in Wiltshire, had their own representative in Parliament. Of the 514 representatives in the UK Parliament, 370 were selected by just 180 rich patrons. Bribery was common: one Grampound voter claimed that he received 300 guineas for his vote, the equivalent of £29,000 today. Just 3 per cent of the 8 million population of England and Wales had the franchise.[12]

The voting system was updated by Parliament through the Great Reform Act of 1832 in response to pressure. The rules of democracy changed. New laws created fairer representation for the communities of the country, abolishing 143 small borough constituencies, such as Grampound, Dunwich and Old Sarum, and giving 22 large towns in England and Wales two representatives each where they previously had one or none. All men with wealth of £10 a year or more were able to vote, so that tailors and shoemakers, as well as landowners and traders, had influence over decision-making for the first time. This increased the total electorate to 650,000 voters. Electoral registers and courts were established to ensure fairness. And from 1835, taxpayers also elected representatives to town councils that were given the power to collect money to meet the needs of the local poor.

Further changes to the rules of democracy were made in the Reform Act of 1884, when the right to vote was extended to 60 per cent of adult men. This meant that poor tenant crofters in Scotland were able to elect representatives to stop evictions from land they had farmed for generations. It was not until 1918 that the long campaign by women to win equal rights achieved limited success, when women over the age of 30 with property were given the vote. Full equality was enacted in the UK in 1928 when all women and men over the age of 21 became eligible to vote, regardless of whether they owned property or not.

These changes to the rules of democracy updated the way communities were represented. The changed rules gave the right to vote to all adult members of a community, made the geography of electoral districts more equal, and put systems in place to ensure fair elections. The rule changes reflected the social changes that had already taken place. Populations had increased, cities had formed, middle classes had expanded, and women had participated alongside men in the First World War. Communities had come together to fight, and millions had paid with their lives.

Those who survived war and sacrifice expected something in return. They particularly wanted public services to address the 'five evils' of squalor, ignorance, want, idleness and disease, as they were memorably labelled in the 1941 Beveridge report.[13] The result was a postwar expansion in public services, with support provided from the cradle to the grave. It included, in 1944, free education for all children under the age of 15. Financial allowances were paid to all families with children from 1946. A National Health Service was established in 1948. And legal aid was put in place in 1949 to give greater access to legal advice. These public services were paid for in part by increased National Insurance contributions, which were made obligatory in 1948.

By 1970, our grandparents expected a wide range of public services to be universally available. They accepted paying around 33 per cent of their income in taxes. In return they expected decent healthcare, education, physical protection and sanitation. Expectations had been raised first by the consequences of the Industrial Revolution and then by the demands of two world wars. Greater participation in the workplace and better education raised expectations higher. These changes in expectations are represented graphically in Figure 2.1.

The economic and social turbulence of the Industrial Revolution brought higher expectations that led those excluded from decision-making to demand changes to the rules of democracy. The rules then changed, allowing more adults to participate in decision-making. This, in turn, helped to reform public services and to meet new social needs. From start to finish, this cycle of change took a century. The Global Technological Revolution sets us a parallel challenge.

Democracy cannot evolve as it did before

However, the solutions of 200 years ago cannot be applied today. First, we are unlikely to accept slow change. Our great-great-grandmothers waited generations for the vote; we do not have the same time to prevent environmental damage. The Global Technological Revolution has also made us less patient. When buying online, we switch at whim from one seller to another. We may want to switch politicians as easily: Japanese voters unexpectedly elected the Democratic Party in 2009, UKIP broke traditional party allegiances from 2013, and French voters switched allegiance to La République en Marche! in 2016. The speed of technological change has made us less loyal to brands. Why should we vote for the same political party all our life, as our grandparents did?

Figure 2.1: Expectations of public services rise following the Industrial Revolution

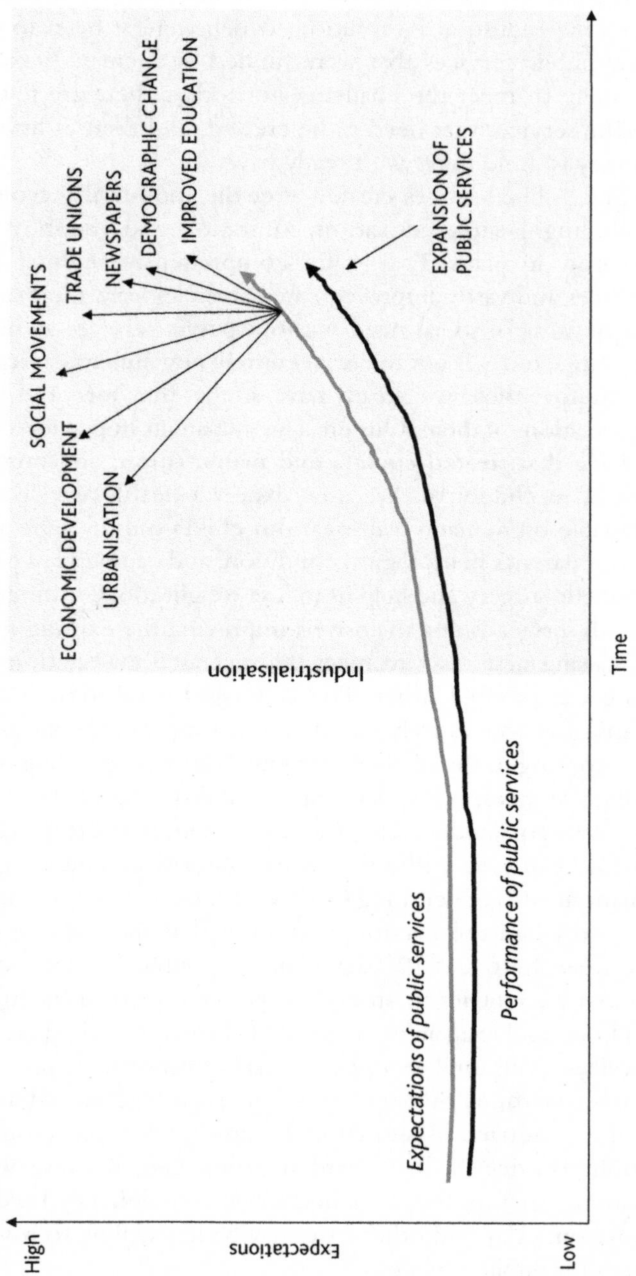

Moreover, the solutions of the past to the social problems arising from the Industrial Revolution, which were at heart to create new public services that were funded by increased taxes, are unlikely to meet the challenges of today: there are few new public services that need to be created, and there is little new money to fund those we already have.

The public services created after the Industrial Revolution, including health, education, sanitation and transportation, are now in place. Except for comprehensive mental health services and vastly improved care for the elderly, there are few major areas of social need without public services at all. The challenge today is not to create entirely new public services, but to improve those we already have, so that they meet our higher expectations of them. Our great-grandparents hoped for a health service that treated cholera and malnutrition, and prevented deaths in childbirth. We now expect a health service that is available on demand, can treat our child's tummy ache as well as our parent's neurological condition, and can perhaps provide cosmetic surgery and help us to lose weight too. Creating a new health service is not an answer; improving the existing one is.

Raising new taxes to meet the increased expectations is no longer as possible either. This is not just because the financial crisis of 2008 massively cut the money spent on public services – according to the Institute for Fiscal Studies, spending on UK public services, particularly on the police, the courts, prisons and transport, reduced by over 10 per cent in the three years to 2015.[14] But even without financial austerity and the long-term financial costs of defeating COVID-19, many communities may have reached the maximum amount that they can be taxed. Between 1910 and 1980, spending on public services doubled in many countries to around 40 per cent of total income.[15] It will not double again to 80 per cent. In fact, spending on public services seems unlikely to exceed half of national income except during wartime. Since 1980, public spending has stabilised in many countries, as shown in Figure 2.2.[16] More money for public services will be hard to find. And, because we pay nothing up front for the online services provided by Facebook, Amazon, eBay and others, we may be less willing to pay more taxes for public services.

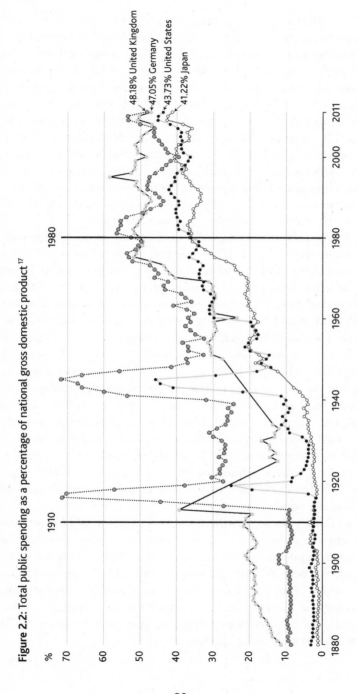

Figure 2.2: Total public spending as a percentage of national gross domestic product[17]

Since 1980, the UK and other countries have tried to improve the efficiency of existing public services, to get more from less. Management techniques and technology have been imported from the commercial world. And some public services have been sold entirely to bring in money and the hope that they will be run better by business. Some of this has worked. Between 2012 and 2018, for example, the number of rail journeys in the UK increased from 360 million to 450 million a year, an increase of 25 per cent, while fatalities and major injuries on the railways remained stable, at under 650 incidents a year. In the same period, the amount of taxpayers' money received by the railways declined by 15 per cent per passenger.[18] Some say that this shows our railways are more efficient.

But improvements in public services have failed to keep pace with increased expectations. The punctuality of some trains, for example, has declined from an average of 98 per cent to 83 per cent. And ticket prices have gone up by over 3 per cent a year, above inflation. Maybe our railways are not more efficient after all. And some efficiency improvements are one-offs. Once we have sold a public asset, such as a bridge, a hospital car park or a railway company, we cannot sell it again, and it will be expensive to buy it back. Similarly, while efficiencies will be found the first time we review the passport application process, the second and third reviews will yield fewer, smaller gains, so the pace of improvement slows. And the efficiencies available to commercial firms are harder to implement in public services. Private sector firms sell our personal data; public services cannot. We do not want schools to sell children's data to advertisers of soft drinks or toys, or doctors to sell our health data to pharmaceutical companies.

Making regular, marginal improvements to public services is important, but these improvements alone cannot meet our higher expectations. As such, the Expectation Gap between what we want from public services and what we get continues to widen. And because we may benchmark our expectations against the relentless increases in performance of online firms, even if public services are improving, they may not improve fast enough to close the Expectation Gap.

Time to change the rules

The Global Technological Revolution is just as dramatic, far-reaching and long-lasting in its social and economic impact as the Industrial Revolution. Both created a gap in expectations of public services. Both led people to clamour for greater influence in the decision-making process. In the case of the Industrial Revolution, the rules of democracy eventually changed. New democratic institutions were created, the franchise was extended and laws were passed to promote greater equality between all members of a community.

Our challenge now is to find ways for the rules of democracy to respond to the new challenges of the Global Technological Revolution. This cannot be done in the same ways as in the past, because the problems are not the same. We still want public services to meet our needs, but we have become more demanding, and our needs are more complex. In addition, we must now tackle complex environmental challenges and the lack of governance of an online world that did not exist even a few decades ago.

The current rules of democracy have served us well enough for the last 100 years, but democracy has yet to find answers to today's challenges. Instead of taking an authoritarian path, we can find ways for the rules of democracy to evolve to enable decision-making in our communities to become stronger, and to harness the power of technology to help improve public services and protect the environment.

Changing the rules of democracy is hard, because any change takes influence away from some and gives it to others. Those benefiting from the current rules resist change. But the demands on the current rules of democracy are becoming impossible to ignore, whether we look at the rise of populism, the damage taking place to the environment or the unregulated global tech monopolies.

In each of the following chapters, a new rule of democracy is suggested as one way for democracy to evolve to meet today's global decision-making challenges. All the rules are listed in the Appendix. Each suggested new rule may today be thought preposterous, but perhaps no more preposterous than when, 250 years ago, Thomas Jefferson and Mary Wollstonecraft declared that all people are born with equal rights.[19]

3

Democracy as a system

I have argued in previous chapters that democracy is the best way for communities to make complex decisions, but that the rules of democracy need to evolve to respond to the current challenges of the Global Technological Revolution. The remainder of the book proposes how that might be done, with new rules to supplement those outlined earlier.

It took hundreds of years to reach some consensus on the existing rules of democracy. Agreeing new ones will be just as difficult, even if the first additional rule of democracy is in some ways obvious:

Elected representatives should exist at every level where decisions are taken that impact on the represented communities, whether these decisions are taken locally, nationally or internationally.

The rule is not entirely new, of course. For centuries, politicians have been elected to local and national bodies to discuss issues and make decisions. Londoners elect 1,836 councillors to 33 local councils to agree issues relating to education, housing, environmental planning, public health and much else, and they elect a single London mayor to manage city-wide transport, major development, business promotion and crime reduction, as well as 73 MPs to debate national issues in Parliament. The residents of Cincinnati, Cologne and Curitiba similarly choose politicians to represent them at local, regional and national levels, and to make decisions on their behalf.

This rule of democracy generally works well enough. We elect politicians and give them authority to decide certain policy issues within a specific geographical boundary. A mayor can manage a city's sewerage, but cannot take decisions *beyond* this remit, such as about a different city or national issues. Similarly, national politicians mostly have no authority to take decisions *below* their geographical or policy remit, such as in relation to a town's roadworks or street lighting, where local politicians are largely authorised to take decisions on behalf of residents. If we want to reduce traffic in our town centre or to improve the disposal of household waste, we elect politicians locally to sort these problems out. And we elect regional or national politicians to address wider-ranging issues such as improving railways or air quality.

This rule of democracy, also known as the principle of subsidiarity,[1] has the potential to bring clarity and effectiveness to decision-making about communities. Indeed, it is a longstanding feature of many democracies. It was observed by Alexis de Tocqueville in the US in the 19th century, and it is core to the functioning of the EU, where Article 3 of the 1992 Treaty of Rome states that decision-making is elevated above national level 'only if and insofar as the objectives of the proposed action cannot be sufficiently achieved [nationally] by reason of [its] scale or effects'. In all countries with a federal structure, certain activities are reserved for counties, provinces or states, while other matters are for action at a national level. In Germany, there are 16 federated states, known as *Länder*, responsible for culture, education and job creation, as well as 402 districts responsible for roads, hospitals and public utilities, and 12,141 local municipalities with responsibility for youth programmes and public health. The same rule applies within the UK, where many issues, including health, education and culture, are devolved for decision-making to the Parliaments of Scotland and Wales and the Northern Ireland Assembly.

Without the clarity provided by this rule of democracy, accountability becomes unclear when things go wrong. Politicians can pass the buck, blaming others at local or national level for policy or operational failure. Local politicians may allege that national funding was inadequate, while national politicians complain that local leadership was weak. In the meantime, communities may remain with inadequate public services and no one taking responsibility for improving them.

In contrast, when this rule of democracy is more clearly understood and well operated, public services can become better managed. Successful international businesses put this rule into effect too. A local supervisor may be responsible for making products in a specific factory on time and to budget, but marketing decisions may be made nationally. Other decisions about manufacturing, branding and distribution may be made globally to ensure overall efficiency and quality. All parts of the company try to communicate with each other as effectively as possible towards achieving shared goals. This is the basis of good corporate governance and represented in case studies in every business school.[2]

The principle is no different for democracies. We give authority, through our vote, to the politicians who are best placed to make decisions about specific issues relevant to our community.

Yet some issues cannot be resolved at local or national level because they are global, including the issues outlined earlier, such as international criminals evading justice, multinational companies avoiding taxation, damage to the environment, unfair global trade, unchecked immigration and unregulated technology firms.

In the governance of a major company, these issues could be addressed at the firm's international headquarters. But in the governance of our communities, we are missing that global layer. Most democracies elect politicians at local and national levels, but none directly elects, and then holds to account, politicians to agree issues that can only be addressed internationally.

For any system to be effective, whether that system is a logistics chain, a piece of software or the governance of our communities, each component in the system is necessary and important. If one part is missing, the whole system can fail.[3] A new house must have its windows and doors firmly fitted, and the water pipes, heating and electricity correctly installed. A well-built house is a complete system, with the hot water regulated by thermostats and the electricity supply by fuses. We are kept warm and dry inside. But if the roof has a hole, or a pipe leaks, then the whole house is compromised. We may end up cold or wet, whichever room we are in.

Like any system, the good governance of our communities requires all parts to work effectively together, including the parts that are local, national or international. The local and national parts of the system of democratic governance are well developed. We have worked on them for centuries. Not so the international layer. This is understandable, as in the 14th century, the Aztecs in Central America, the Ming dynasty in China and the medieval Italian city states could co-exist with little or no impact on each other. Thanks to globalisation, that will never be true again. Our world is interconnected as never before. We know, for example, that the world's environment is a complex connected system of air, heat and water that can be imperilled in any location across the planet. The same applies to financial markets. The internet is a complex global system too. Changing one part of any of these systems will impact on other parts in ways that can be hard to predict. We have seen this in runs on financial markets after 2008, and in the management of the COVID-19 pandemic from 2020.

The way we make decisions in our communities today is akin to living in a house with holes in the roof. Some important issues that affect us can only be resolved internationally, but the existing ways of resolving these issues are inadequate, partly because they are not democratic. This results in poorer decisions, as most of those impacted by the decisions cannot inform decision-makers about the possible impacts of their choices. And the decisions are likely to be less legitimate, too, when most communities are excluded from representation in decision-making processes.

Improving international decision-making

Communities have long recognised that some issues require cross-border cooperation. The ancient empires of Egypt, Babylon, India and China each had common currencies to ensure commercial exchanges were fair. Official coins changed hands around the Aegean Sea over 2,700 years ago, and international trade along the old Silk Road and within pre-Colombian Central America required standard weights and measures so that different communities could do business on an equitable basis. International trade agreements have been put in place ever since. In 1995, 124 countries created the World Trade Organization, built from the 1947 General Agreement on Tariffs and Trades, so that there could be fair rules to regulate the trade in goods, services and intellectual property, and to resolve disputes neutrally and objectively.

Cross-border collaborative action has taken place on other fronts. There are 192 member countries of Interpol, the International Criminal Police Organisation, which tackles international cyber-crime, intellectual property theft, money laundering and the smuggling of drugs, weapons and people. In 2015, 195 counties signed the Paris Agreement to reduce the impact of greenhouse gas emissions and to limit global warming.

Some countries have gone further, forming wider-ranging pacts. Argentina, Brazil, Paraguay and Uruguay formed the Mercosur common market in 1991, while Canada, Mexico and the US formed a similar North American Free Trade Agreement, NAFTA, in 1994. The Association of South East Asian Nations (ASEAN) has encouraged mutual cooperation on economic, political, military, educational and cultural issues among its 10 members since 1967, and the EU of now 27 countries has promoted shared political, economic, trading, cultural and developmental goals since 1958. And 193 countries are members of the UN, which tries to maintain international order, including through its agencies such as the International Court of Justice, the World Bank, the World Health Organization (WHO), the International Atomic Energy Agency (IAEA) and its culture and education agency, UNESCO.

These organisations, comprising sovereign states, make decisions through haggling and trade-offs among their members. The International Organization for Standardization, for example, is run by a council of 20 national standards bodies that reports to a general assembly of all 161 member countries. The UN itself has an assembly of its 193 members overseen by a president elected from among them. Each country has one vote, but its resolutions are not binding. Its Security Council, which tries to keep international peace, has 15 members, including as permanent members China, France, Russia, the UK and US, and 10 other countries sitting for two years each. The WHO has an executive board of 34 health ministers, but it is an assembly of delegates from 194 countries that decides its policies and budget and appoints its director-general.

This governance model of haggling and trade-offs often results in large, rich or powerful countries trying to persuade small, poor or weaker countries to support proposals in return for favours or deals elsewhere. This is the realpolitik of international diplomacy, where morals or ethics may be secondary to more pragmatic considerations.[4]

The EU is the only international body that has a directly elected parliament of 705 representatives elected by its 400 million voters. But even here, these politicians have limited power and cannot propose new laws. Instead, it is the European Council of 27 national politicians that sets overall priorities, while a European Commission of administrators turn the objectives into draft laws, which are then approved by councils of national ministers, with the parliament having a more minor role.

Thus, while there are multiple mechanisms for communities to collaborate extensively across their own borders to make decisions on issues that none can resolve individually, the current global decision-making processes are not wholly democratic, and decision-makers are not directly accountable. This means that if democracy is accepted as likely to be a better way to make complex decisions across multiple communities, then the decisions currently made internationally risk having less legitimacy than those made democratically, and may, indeed, be worse than if they had been made by democratically elected politicians on behalf of the communities they represent. Decisions may favour richer, more powerful nations over others, and thus be suboptimal for the world as a whole.

Accountability for global decision-makers is lacking. It is difficult to identify who makes international decisions now. Most decision-makers have been appointed by national governments, perhaps for political reasons or because they have a particular nationality. This is how top appointments at the UN,

NATO (North Atlantic Treaty Organization) and EU are made. When there is no agreement, a job can go to the least offensive candidate available. In 1998, the first head of the European Central Bank, Wim Duisenberg, was a compromise candidate from the Netherlands who was the least disliked by the Germans and the Southern Europeans. In 2019, Ursula von der Leyen was appointed to be president of the European Commission because she raised the fewest objections among Europe's powerbrokers.[5]

Selecting people on the basis of who knows whom, and without fair or open competition, inevitably risks putting weak, inexperienced or corrupt people into important decision-making roles. Even when the appointed decision-makers are knowledgeable and honest, they still owe their allegiance to those who appointed them, acting in the interests of their sponsors when striking deals. As they are not elected, they are not accountable to the communities impacted by their decisions.

In contrast, in democracies at local and national level, politicians debate issues in public, and try to represent fully and fairly the opinions of the communities who gave them power. They scrutinise and challenge the decisions made by public bodies, requesting more detailed information when necessary. None of this happens internationally. The way that international bodies make decisions is secret. We rarely know whether decision-makers considered evidence or were influenced by lobbying, as these bodies are unaccountable and generally also lack transparency. Technical decisions need not be publicly explained, as they must be in more accountable legislatures. This, in turn, makes it easier for lobby groups to achieve hidden influence. Over half of the €160 billion annual budget of the EU is spent on subsidies and cash transfers to those who have successfully (and mostly invisibly) lobbied for the money, including 37 per cent to EU farmers.[6]

Smaller and poorer countries get a bad deal from the current international arrangements. In contrast, democratic decision-making at national level gives all communities, however poor, the potential for influence: MPs in the UK represent deprived coastal towns as much as rich city suburbs. International decisions, however, are mostly made by a few rich countries, reflecting power relationships from 100 years ago. Combined, the powerful G7 countries plus Russia have 28 per cent of the world's population but 51 per cent of its wealth. The six countries of Indonesia, India, Pakistan, Nigeria, Bangladesh and Brazil have the same combined population, but collectively only 15 per cent of the world's wealth. The views of people in these countries are unlikely to prevail if the US, Russia and China agree to a decision, whatever its impact elsewhere. Yet all communities across the globe must trade and buy goods according to common standards, use the internet, and benefit from a planet with sustainable oceans and unpolluted air.

Haggling and trade-offs, of course, take place in decision-making in democracies at a national level too. Every trade-off involves a sacrifice, with something given up in order to achieve something else. But in a democracy at a national or local level, the deals tend to be more visible. And those who agree to the deals are later accountable to those who elected them: they can be challenged and ultimately removed from office if the deals are unwelcome or go sour. But for international decisions, we generally do not know who is making decisions, how or when decisions are made, or what trade-offs are taking place. And even with this information, there is little we can do to influence decisions or hold those making them to account. This is a manifestation of the Accountability Gap. It fuels the suspicion that we are helpless against the vested interests of a powerful world elite who make decisions only for their own benefit.

International democracy

It is nonetheless possible for communities to take back control of global decision-making. Not by leaving international decision-making clubs, whether the EU or Paris climate accords, as this may only reduce a country's ability to influence decision-making. Instead, the system of governance and decision-making can be made to work better overall by addressing the 'hole in the roof' at an international level. This means applying the rule of democracy as much to an international level as to local and national levels. This would allow communities to choose politicians to argue for their interests and hold decision-makers to account internationally as much as they do locally and nationally. It would help make any necessary trade-offs and sacrifices more visible, with decisions potentially made more fairly and in the interests of all the communities of the world, and not just the economic or military powerhouses.

We are far from being able to directly elect politicians to represent us in a global parliament. Indeed, the chances of doing so in the short term are nil, despite good work by the Inter-Parliamentary Union and others to establish a UN parliamentary assembly. But to create a more comprehensive and effective system of global governance, that can make more representative, more transparent and more accountable decisions, this is what is required. It means a directly elected world parliament, as has been mooted since the creation of the League of Nations in 1919 and more recently by philosophers such as Jürgen Habermas and others.[7]

The many practical obstacles aside, a world parliament could draw on good democratic practice learned over 2,000 years. Just as in national democracies, it should ensure everyone is equally represented, with every adult on the planet having an equal vote in selecting politicians to make decisions on global issues. This is in line with the first rule of democracy – that 'people are born with equal rights, including to freedom and safety from harm'.

The number of representatives must be enough for adequate representation from all communities, but not so many as to be unwieldy. Germany has 598 representatives in its Bundestag, the EU has 705 MEPs, and India has 543 representatives in the Lok Sabha, its lower chamber. In a global parliament, this might mean one politician for every 10 million people, creating a parliament of around 770 members. Representing the views of 10 million people is challenging, but no more than is currently being asked of the mayors of London and New York or the leaders of Portugal, Sweden and Hungary. On this basis, the people of the US would elect 32 representatives and the UK 7. The people of China would elect 140, including 2 from Beijing and 9 from Hong Kong and Guangdong. Indonesia would have 26, Brazil 21, Bangladesh 16, Ethiopia 10 and so on. The neighbouring countries of Costa Rica and Panama could elect a representative between them, as might Norway and Denmark combined.

The boundaries of world constituencies would require extensive consultation, led by an independent commission, modelled on national Boundary Commissions.[8] Their decisions would need to take account of population density, the way that communities define themselves, existing administrative districts and physical geography. Existing mapping software and population survey data would make this easier than ever before. Yet, although difficult, establishing 770 global democratic constituencies would ensure that each community in the world could have its own politician, with equal rights to champion their interests when international decisions are made. This would be fairer than today's governance model of haggling and trade-offs between powerful nation-states, where the voice of much of the world is marginalised.

The other rules of democracy would apply internationally too. There would need to be regular and free elections to choose representatives, which is hard to imagine in many countries at present. And the parliament would need a place to meet, perhaps in a city that is as accessible to as many countries as possible. To put its decisions into effect, a global parliament, like any national parliament, would have control over its own institutions. In a global setting, this means the UN bodies, making them immediately more accountable for their decisions. The UN costs US\$5.4 billion each year to run now, currently raised from national governments. A global parliament would need to fund its activity, as national parliaments do. This might be through a tax on global businesses and technology firms, or by fining environmental polluters. Establishing a transparent global tax, imposed by accountable politicians, might reduce global tax evasion by large firms and international criminals, address inequities in the global finance system, as argued by economist Thomas Piketty, and mitigate or reduce CO_2 emissions.[9]

A global parliament could strengthen the rules-based world, with international issues debated and agreed with greater transparency and accountability than now. Its remit would be limited to issues best decided only at a global level, including international trade and commerce, the taxation of international business, cross-border crime, the environment, management of the oceans, regulation of the internet and standard-setting for international products and services. Decisions in other areas would remain for politicians to agree at national or local level.

Applying this rule of democracy at an international level would retain the current benefits of international cooperation, allowing interested parties to discuss common problems, including complex social and environmental issues that cannot be solved by individual countries alone. It would, in addition, allow everyone impacted by global issues to be fairly represented when decisions are made. It could make international decision-makers more accountable, limiting the risk that hidden benefits are given to the influential. International law could become more legitimate and enforceable, and harder for criminals or global companies or polluters to avoid.

It may improve world leadership too. Currently, national politicians often see no domestic benefit in sorting out a mess beyond their shores, whether that is poverty or migration or environmental damage. This leaves a leadership vacuum. Accountable global politicians would have no option but to fill that gap, working together to find solutions, responding dynamically to change to meet their constituents' needs. Democracy, with its ability to allow us to regularly reflect our changing aspirations and expectations by voting for different politicians to represent us internationally, would forge a more responsive and sophisticated governance system than the current rigid global governance arrangements that have not changed since 1945.

A global parliament, even if accepted in theory, is unrealistic in practice in the short term. Opponents of international democracy would include those opposed to democracy itself who dislike governance models that involve debate and compromise. Rich countries would lose power relative to others if decision-making influence were more fairly distributed. Global companies would also be losers if they become subject to more consistent cross-border regulation and tax regimes that could bring in billions to fund public services. Existing international bodies, including the UN and its agencies, will resist becoming more accountable.

But the global status quo is not coping well with the challenges created by the Global Technological Revolution, and we should not be content to stick with the 20th-century world order. Three thousand years ago, there were around 600,000 independent, autonomous political communities on the planet. Today, the world has under 200 countries. Alliances and war brought people together over time into larger groups as they realised that they could address more complex issues by working together. In Europe, the 1648 Peace of Westphalia temporarily ended religious and territorial wars by establishing co-existing sovereign states that agreed not to interfere in each other's domestic affairs. These arrangements worked well enough for 400 years. But they are now no longer sufficient to address today's cross-cutting, international challenges. .

We need not leave these challenges to be resolved through conflict. Instead, rules-based democracy can forge a comprehensive if complex system that enables people to discuss contentious issues within a formal process that allows for dialogue, discussion, compromise and agreement. Applying the rules of democracy internationally will help to reduce global conflict by giving every community the ability to choose someone to represent them in decisions that impact on their lives. Global decision-making can become more transparent and accountable, and we may come to have greater confidence that those we elect to represent us will make decisions with our interests in mind, and take responsibility for their decisions too.

Local democracy

International democracy is not, however, the only way to improve our system of governance and to narrow the Accountability Gap between those who make those decisions and us. This, and the Expectation Gap between what we want from public services and what we actually get, can also be closed by improving local democracy.

We mainly experience the world locally, not internationally. We wake each morning to the sounds of our neighbourhood; we open our front door and see the buildings and roads around us; we travel to work; we buy food; we send our children to school; and we visit our doctor. All this happens locally. In fact, we spend most of our week within two hours of our own bed, and almost half of us are likely to live within 50 miles of where we were born. Even in the US, with its history of internal migration, 54 per cent of people live close to where they grew up and, on average, 18 miles from their parents.[10] In other less wealthy countries, people stay even more local. Most of the world does not have a passport and has never travelled abroad.

So, while we increasingly connect digitally with a global world through the internet, we actually live most of our physical lives in our local community. We experience most public services locally too. We care about our local schools and clinics, and we grumble about the state of the roads or how the rubbish is collected. We want local buses and trains to be regular and cheap. And we want clean air and local open spaces to enjoy too.

These public services are not only experienced locally, but also provided locally. A local high street may have a publicly funded library, school or care home. Doctors, teachers, firefighters and council workers often live in their local community too.

This means that local democracy matters. Politicians know this. US Speaker Tip O'Neill (1912–94) was among many to declare that 'All politics is local'. This makes it important for us to choose local politicians who can represent our interests when decisions about local public services are made. We choose these politicians from among us and may even know them personally. In many democracies, from the UK to Australia, they each represent around 4,000 local people. They are thus well placed to understand local aspirations and concerns. They see the strengths and weaknesses of local public services, respond to changing local demographics, try to make peace between conflicting local views, and know who to lobby and what to say in order to make positive change happen locally.

Effective local democracy shortens the time between problems being identified and solutions being found. Local democracy allows us to meet someone face to face on our own high street to discuss our concerns. Homelessness in Manchester will rarely be solved by bureaucrats in London. Local knowledge pays dividends.

Yet, despite the importance of local democracy in theory, many people are dissatisfied with it in practice, and suspicious that local politicians can do little to improve public services in their community. Such concerns feed the Expectation Gap about public services. If we expect public services akin to the high-quality commercial services we receive online, but actually experience underfunded or underperforming public services locally, our confidence in the ability of local democracy to respond to our needs will be damaged.

Many have argued that stronger local democracy is an effective way for local social needs to be met, and that local democratic bodies, including councils, should be given more power and more money.[11] The long-recognised problem is that the local tier of democracy in the UK has little formal responsibility for many important local public services. Hospitals, social services and road maintenance are managed at county level or regionally, while most housing and school policies are set nationally. There is often little that local politicians can do to improve public services, even if they want to.

This means applying the new rule of democracy locally as much as internationally, so politicians make decisions where they are best placed to do so, whether that is locally, nationally or internationally. For local politicians to make a difference, they must have genuine authority over, and accountability for, the public services that are provided locally, rather than be passive against decisions made elsewhere. This requires responsibility for local public services to start locally. This would include primary and secondary education, clinics and hospitals, social care, housing, street cleaning, road building and local environmental issues. This would allow local politicians better to determine how to meet the needs of their own community and to be accountable for their decisions.

Local mayors are an example of how this can be effective in practice. They provide visible local leadership, and accountability for local public services. They often have authority over essential public services, including health, education, waste collection and transport. The World Mayor prize celebrates those who have led their local communities well, with winners including mayors from Athens, Melbourne and Bilbao. In 2018, the prize was won by Valeria Mancinelli, mayor of Ancona in Italy, after she helped to revive local shipbuilding and brought manufacturing jobs to her town. Mayors are not the only way to strengthen local democracy, however; all politicians elected locally should have the power to be effective.

But there is a second problem for local democracy apart from the lack of power. Local democracy lacks money. That local public services need more money is an easy and frequent complaint, but those elected locally are often highly constrained in how they can raise money to fund local public services, even if they are responsible for them. This is because, in the UK and elsewhere, tax collection is often centralised and controlled at a national level. Local government then relies on grants from national government, which are never generously given, while having limited legal power to raise taxes or generate income locally themselves. The problem is acute in the UK where, in 2018–19, only a third of the money spent by local councils on their own services was raised locally, representing less than 8 per cent of total public spending. In contrast, in Switzerland, the power to raise taxes is primarily with cantons, which are communities of between 16,000 and 1.5 million people. They can raise direct taxes on incomes, as well as on inheritance, property and vehicles, accounting for 40 per cent of all Swiss taxes raised. This has the potential to make local democracy far more responsive to local people and businesses, and better able to understand and meet their needs.[12]

For the system of democracy to work effectively overall, local politicians should be better able to raise and keep taxes from their community so that they can fund the public services that they are responsible for, while recognising that some areas will have a stronger tax base than others, and that some transfer of funds between communities will be necessary to ensure wider fairness across community boundaries.

This would mean giving more responsibility to local politicians. But this is hard when they are already overworked and underpaid. In the UK, there are over 20,000 local councillors. They work on average 22 hours a week, with 19 per cent working more than 31 hours a week, and 40 per cent holding down full-time jobs on top of their democratic responsibilities. Representing a community effectively is demanding. It is also poorly paid. Local councillors get no salary at all, although they can claim an allowance. In Herefordshire, this amounts to £2,454 a year, in Swansea it is £13,300 a year, and in the Scottish Highlands, it is £16,900. Some small councils only reimburse travel costs. Meanwhile, the average annual income across the UK is £28,700. Instead, local politicians should be paid a salary. They are accountable for taking important decisions on behalf of communities. They spend hours listening to local residents, and then make difficult decisions on everyone's behalf. If they are not paid, we should not be surprised that so few people stand for election, and that those who do are not fully representative of our communities.[13]

It is easier to hold politicians to account if they are closer to us, represent fewer people and better understand the local public services we rely on. This means putting local democracy first. Strong, accountable local democracy can help to close the Expectation Gap between what we want from local public services and what we get. Local needs will differ in Wick, Walthamstow and Weston-super-Mare. The way local decisions are taken may also differ from place to place. But local democracy is a key part of the democratic system overall. Decision-making about important issues is connected, as in any system. This means, in a democracy, appropriate responsibility locally as well as nationally, with local politicians having the power and money to make and implement decisions to improve local public services that matter in each community. Their jobs are important, just as are those of national politicians, and should be appropriately remunerated. Local politicians should be held to account for their decisions too. Often, we do not know who is accountable for our local public services, and we cannot question them or vote them out of office. Without such a rule of democracy being implemented, the current Accountability Gap, between those who make decisions and us, and the Expectation Gap, between what we want from public services and what we get, will remain.

National democracy

Applying a rule of democracy to establish international politicians with the authority and accountability to address global issues, and giving stronger authority and accountability to local politicians to improve public services, will help to resolve the problem identified by sociologist Daniel Bell in 1987, that 'the nation-state is becoming too small for the big problems of life, and too big for the small problems of life'.[14] But many important issues still need to be decided by politicians elected at a national level.

Many commercial services involve a mix of geographies. There is no need for an airport or car part distribution centre in each local community. Similarly, some public services do not need to be on our doorstep. Major public infrastructure such as railways, canals and flood defences fall into this category, as do aspects of healthcare and education that are not used regularly, including medical units to treat severe burns and university archaeology departments.

Decisions about these public services are made by national politicians who are best placed to understand the national issues involved and to make decisions and be accountable for them. Their responsibilities also include many aspects of economic, industrial and trade policy. They ensure that the needs of the national community are met, and that individual local communities cannot act selfishly in their own narrow interests, such as by dumping their sewage into a river for others to suffer from downstream, or by failing to maintain flood defences on their stretch of coastline.

But some commercial services, like the sale of food and drink, are experienced locally yet organised regionally or nationally for economies of scale. This makes sense for firms, so that they improve consistency of service and save money.

The same economies of scale apply to public services. Even very local public services, such as primary schools, have features that can be managed more cheaply at a national level, such as the training of teachers or the design of a curriculum. But commercial logic and a focus only on efficiency has led decision-making about local public services to drift further away from local communities, with decisions made by national politicians who are generally less well placed to understand the needs of each local community and to make appropriate decisions on their behalf. This sustains the Accountability Gap between decision-makers and us, and can cause frustration with democracy's apparent inability to respond to social needs.

Instead, we should presume that public services are accountable to the layer of democracy where the services are experienced most. If a public service is used exclusively locally, whether GPs, schools, libraries, youth centres or street cleaning, then democratic responsibility could be with local politicians too, even if they contract with national providers. If, on the other hand, public services cross local boundaries, as with travel on trains and roads, or specialist medical provision, or universities, then democratic responsibility could remain at a national level.

In other words, accountability as well as efficiency could inform who takes political decisions on behalf of communities. Making clear who is responsible for managing and improving public services by applying this rule of democracy will help to increase the accountability of politicians, and make public services more responsive to communities' needs, helping democracy to work better as a system overall.

Implementing a more holistic system of democracy would allocate decision-making responsibilities more appropriately between politicians elected locally, nationally and internationally. It would be a more complex system of democracy, but one that reflects the reality of our world following the changes of the Global Technological Revolution. We experience some issues locally, some nationally and some internationally. A system of democracy that does not include international representation, and which does not recognise that some public services are experienced locally and others nationally, cannot accurately take account of the complex nature of the overlapping geographies that we experience most days of our life. We want the street outside our front door to be clean, the regional trains to run on time, and the global internet to keep our personal data secure. We need political representatives at local, national and international levels, making decisions effectively within their remits as part of an overall system, to make sure all this happens.

Matters of the heart

There are, however, other issues that politicians discuss that do not relate to public services. If practical issues relating to national and local services might be termed 'matters of the head', then we also ask politicians to resolve our 'matters of the heart'. These relate to identity and history, and tend to be less easy to sort out with logic and objectivity. Yet they can be as important as any improvement to public services, and often more so. Our history and our identity are deeply personal, and we usually want to protect them fiercely.

We define ourselves in many ways. One is by geography. If a person says they are French or Nicaraguan, their description implies a physical place. And they may indeed live in France or Nicaragua. But these words describe more than a country, and also bring to mind a language, a history and set of customs, even when the person lives elsewhere.

Geographical identities may be local or regional, as well as national. The UK has many overlapping identities within its nations, with our personal geography an important part of our identity. These geographical identities are represented by the politicians we elect on the basis of boundaries drawn around a physical community. A local councillor represents the interests of a neighbourhood; an MP represents the interests of a town, and so on.

But we each have many other identities too. These may be ethnic or religious. They may relate to our sexuality, the way we look, the food we eat, or the music we listen to. These identities overlap. The same person may identify as British, a Londoner, Muslim, a mother, a chemist, a gardener and a tennis fan. All at the same time. We each have our own such labels. The Global Technological Revolution has enabled us to make connections online with others who identify in ways we do, making some existing identities more noticeable and affirming new ones. We can now celebrate shared characteristics with others in online communities wherever we actually live, in ways that we could never do before.[15] This has implications for democratic representation.

It is important that our geographical communities are represented politically. We live in a physical world. Our other diverse identities must also be represented by politicians when decisions are made.

Politicians come from our communities, so they, too, have multiple identities. They may be old or young, or adhere to a particular religion. They may have experienced physical or mental ill health. They may like hunting, shooting and fishing. Or they may prefer camping, walking and birdwatching. Among the politicians who represent us geographically will be some who share our other identities, and who can defend these interests when decisions are made, regardless of whether they represent our own geographical community or not.

All politicians can represent our identities in this way. National politicians are particularly well placed to do so. Local politicians are elected by a few thousand people who may be less diverse than a national community, while international politicians may necessarily be distant from the millions they represent. National politicians, representing perhaps 85,000 people, can help communities to articulate, accept, protect and celebrate identities, histories and customs, whatever these may be. Some politicians may defend a way of life against unwanted change. Others may champion change against a rigid status quo. Collectively, politicians help us to reconcile differences within our communities by debating and trying to agree, on our behalf, what to do about issues of identity that can often be very contentious, with views that are hard to reconcile. Politicians can collectively balance the need to change with the desire to preserve tradition. Their tricky role is to help all parts of a community to agree how to live with change and with the histories and cultures of multiple identities, and without conflict.

Effective democratic representation nationally, within a system of local and international democracy, in line with this new rule of democracy, can help to ensure that all identities are represented. Politicians are leaders of the difficult task of helping communities to preserve as well as adapt their identities through times of change. National politicians are a lynchpin in a complex system of democracy that can link decision-making locally, nationally and internationally, and take account of diverse interests so that complex social, business and environmental issues are resolved despite communities' differing needs, priorities and identities.

The evolution of democracy

In such ways, democracy can evolve as a system to respond to the challenges of the Global Technological Revolution. Directly elected and accountable international politicians can represent our interests on global issues, with stronger local democracy to give us greater influence over decisions about our community, and national politicians to resolve national issues and champion our identities.

Hundreds of years ago, endemic regional conflicts were resolved in part by the formation of nation-states such as Germany, Italy, France and Britain. Yet Bavarians, Tuscans, Bretons and Scots remain rightly proud of their separate regional traditions and histories, while benefiting from a national forum where disputes can be settled and approaches to change agreed. The same evolution could now take place internationally, with accountable politicians from every continent gathering to discuss common problems and finding compromise through debate.

Structuring democracy as a system in this way will give us greater control over the decision-making that impacts on our lives, whether it relates to the cleanliness of the neighbourhood streets or the protection of the oceans, because we could elect someone to represent our interests at each level. Implementing democracy as a global system along these lines may be unrealistic immediately, and begs multiple questions, including about the roles of a global executive and judicial branches of government, in addition to global legislature. But it is a plausible if partial response to the Accountability Gap that has resulted from a globalised, technological, interconnected world. Democracy is an effective way for complex community decisions to be made and for decision-makers to be held to account. Democracy as a system can evolve by adopting a new rule so that 'elected representatives exist at every level where decisions are taken that impact on the represented communities, whether these decisions are taken locally, nationally or internationally'.

4

Paying by the rules

'Nothing can be said to be certain but death and taxes.' So wrote Daniel Defoe in 1726 and Benjamin Franklin in 1789. They were right. All communities, whether democratic or not, have needed to find the resources to pay for communal benefits for its members, whether security against an enemy or sanitation against disease. This is described in a rule of democracy that has already been mentioned:

> [Shared] benefits cost the communities money and effort to provide. Communities raise the money to provide the benefits, mostly by imposing taxes on the people of their own community.

In democracies, politicians are given power by their voters to make decisions on behalf of communities. To be effective, politicians must be able to raise money to implement their decisions. This power to raise and spend our money comes, in a democracy, with accountability to those whose money they are spending. This accountability was enshrined in the UK's 1689 Bill of Rights, and forcibly expressed in 1776 by the American revolutionaries who called for 'no taxation without representation'. Our taxes are supposed to be allocated in our collective interests, to help improve public services and address other issues that are important to us in our communities.

At the moment, however, it is hard to see where our money is actually going. Greater transparency of taxation would help to hold politicians to account for their decisions and close the Accountability Gap between decision-makers and us.

Tax transparency may also help to close the Expectation Gap between what we expect and what we actually get from public services. The impact of the Global Technological Revolution has made it both necessary and possible to suggest a new rule of democracy along the following lines:

> How taxes are raised and spent should be wholly transparent to those paying the taxes, with sufficient tax-raising powers at every democratic level where politicians make spending decisions on behalf of their communities.

Each part of the overall system of democracy should have responsibility for relevant public services, and the power to raise money to fund them. They should each be accountable to voters for spending the money too. Greater tax transparency can help this happen. Currently, poor tax transparency, complex taxes and unclear tax-raising powers cause confusion about tax rules, unfairness in the amounts paid and the services received in return, and loopholes that allow some not to play by the rules at all, by avoiding paying taxes altogether. Playing by the rules of democracy involves paying by the rules too.

The history and purpose of taxation

Taxation has existed since at least Ancient Egypt. Pharaohs toured their kingdoms twice a year to collect a fifth share of all crops, or the labour of those too poor to give up their food. The Romans taxed wealth and property, including land, homes, slaves and animals, at the rate of 1 per cent a year, rising to 3 per cent at times of war. The first modern income tax was introduced in Britain in 1798 to pay for war against France at a rate of 1 per cent on annual incomes of over £60 (around £7,000 today) and up to 10 per cent on incomes over £200 (£26,000 today). Abraham Lincoln signed income tax into law in the US in 1861 at a flat rate of 3 per cent on all income over US$800 (about US$22,500 today).[1]

These funds paid for activities that individuals in a community could not provide on their own. Instead, resources were pooled.

Early taxes were used to raise funds for war so that communities could protect themselves. Later, taxes paid for roads, aqueducts and drainage that brought benefits to whole communities. Today, by pooling our resources through taxation, we share benefits with others in our community. Our children are educated, our sick are treated and our elderly cared for. We travel safely and quickly to work. We enjoy the beauty of our natural environment. And we gather together in public places to appreciate history, music and the arts.

We pool our resources through taxation to stop bad things happening, whether violence, natural disaster, theft, poverty or disease. And we pool our resources to make good things happen too, including economic development, education, transport, clean air, parks and culture. It is easier to see the public goods that our taxes have bought: schools, hospitals and national parks. It is less easy to see the absence of the public bads, although we benefit from them, too. In the UK, we are rarely assaulted on the train or bus, or contract typhoid from contaminated food, or walk past human faeces or dead dogs. These events are avoided in part because, over many decades, politicians have invested our taxes in preventing them or reducing their likelihood.

But few of us like paying taxes. We often try to reduce the amount we pay. Accountants may advise us to put money into our pension or to give money to charity to reduce our taxes. Companies can be creative in their tax avoidance, including by moving profits to different tax jurisdictions to pay as little as possible. Google, Amazon and Facebook pay only 10 per cent tax on their profits in Europe compared to the 23 per cent paid by most other companies. In 2014, Apple sent profits to Ireland where it paid a 0.005 per cent tax rate, 2,500 times less than the 12.5 per cent corporate tax rate. Qualcomm, another tech giant, posted most of its profits in Singapore to get tax breaks, although its business is mostly in China and the West. Amazon posted its profits to Luxembourg for the same reason. Alibaba, a US$56 billion Chinese tech firm, is registered for tax in the Cayman Islands. Over 61 per cent of multinational companies report zero profit in the UK and pay no tax at all. A quarter of all the profits from US multinational companies are posted to low tax countries, depriving US communities of between

US$100 billion and US$155 billion of tax revenue between 2010 and 2019.[2]

These and other firms lobby tax authorities to change tax rules in their favour. It is a big industry. There are 12,000 full-time lobbyists in Washington, DC alone putting their company's case on tax and other issues. In 2019, US$3.5 billion was spent on all lobbying in the US, including US$7 million by Apple.[3] The result is a variety of minor, and not so minor, tax exceptions and exemptions, with rebates to particular companies or to particular products or to particular areas. Common tax exemptions around the world include those for people who are soldiers, religious leaders or who start businesses in poor communities.

As a consequence, those who have more money tend to pay less tax, proportionately, than those who earn less.[4] Yet rich and poor alike benefit from the same roads, public health, crime prevention and rubbish collection that are paid for from everyone's taxes.

There are other ways we avoid tax. We may fail to declare the extra income from renting out a spare room. Or we may pay a builder or a cleaner in cash to avoid sales tax. This kind of tax evasion is illegal in most countries, but it is commonplace, such that 'black markets' can be very large indeed. The underground economy in the US is worth about US$2 trillion a year, or about 5 per cent of all economic activity. In Greece and Italy, the illegal economy is said to amount to as much as 20 per cent of these countries' wealth. In other countries it is higher still, amounting to between a fifth and a quarter of world GDP. As these transactions are untaxed, the individuals involved can benefit financially from the trade between them, while everyone else pays for the cost of creating the legal, economic, social and financial frameworks that make these transactions possible. Those people worth over US$40 million have been found to evade around 30 per cent of their taxes. Worldwide, the IMF estimates that the amount lost to communities from tax avoidance is between US$240 billion and US$600 billion a year.[5]

Taxing a community thus becomes an endless game of hide and seek that pits its members against each other. We may each accept that taxation is necessary in theory, but we don't want to pay much of it ourselves in practice. Tax authorities therefore try to take our money in ways that are hard to spot and harder to avoid. They design the tax system to be complex and opaque, so that, as France's finance minister Jean-Baptiste Colbert said in about 1680, our financial feathers are plucked with as little hissing as possible. Germany has 118 tax laws and 96,000 tax regulations. The US has 1,177 separate tax forms. The complexity creates loopholes around which accountants, lawyers and tax inspectors do battle.

The cost of this game of hide and seek between countries and companies is enormous, both in time and money, with different countries played against each other too. Each taxpayer in the US spends on average 12 hours and US$261 each year on their tax return. In Australia the same process takes each taxpayer 4 hours and AU$170 a year. Multiplied by millions of taxpayers, this is a lot of money. The cost of tax compliance in Germany, where rules are particularly intricate, is €7 billion a year, or about 3.5 per cent of the country's overall tax revenue.[6]

These costs have long been recognised, with many attempts at tax simplification. In the UK, the Chartered Institute of Taxation has worked since 1930 to promote a better, more efficient tax system, and an Office of Tax Simplification was set up in 2010 to give the government advice on the matter, with mixed success. Yet, while there is widespread consensus that tax should be simpler, there is disagreement about how. Simpler taxes may not be fairer for certain groups, and politicians will always find it useful to changes tax codes to achieve their immediate political goals. In the meantime, lawyers and accountants benefit from their US$500 billion industry, and tax authorities miss out on about £31 billion a year in the UK alone.[7]

Tax transparency

The Global Technological Revolution has nonetheless given us new tools to help reduce the complexity and cost of taxation, and new ways to increase the accountability of those who tax us and spend our money. Greater tax transparency may help us see whether our tax contribution is fair and consistent with others' payments, and whether money is being spent reasonably by politicians on our behalf, to benefit communities in ways that its members could not achieve on their own.[8]

The leaders of undemocratic countries have no need to be transparent about how they spend public money. They can even give cash to friends and families and have no obligation to publish accounts or answer to taxpayers. In democracies, in contrast, politicians make decisions on behalf of others, both about the benefits to be provided and how they will be paid for. Their decisions involve taking and spending our money so that the community as a whole can benefit. As a result, we may try to elect politicians whose spending decisions mirror our own, such as a politician who says they will spend money on education rather than on building a new airport, or vice versa. In this way, politicians reflect choices about what we value, including how they tax and spend our money. Public services that are more valuable to us, such as, perhaps, safe streets or protected woodland, are taxed less or receive more funds from public money, while things that we value less, such as, perhaps, gambling or tobacco, are taxed more and may receive no public funding at all. Politicians thus decide how, when and where our money should be spent by asking us via democratic elections and then responding to our views. Because democratic politicians are answerable to their communities, it is harder for them, in theory, to use tax money for their private benefit. And it is easier for them to be held to account for any bad decisions they make.

In practice, however, the current complexity of the tax system and its lack of transparency reduces the accountability of those who make decisions about how taxes are taken and how they are spent. Once we have elected our politicians, we have little knowledge of the decisions they take to tax us and to spend our taxes. We may fear that our money is spent poorly, but we are unlikely to know exactly where or how. This matters. We give politicians power to take lots and lots of our money, and to spend it as they think fit. Yet, at the moment, when politicians tell us that they are spending our money on education or the police, or that there is not enough money for housing or the environment, we have few independent ways to check that they are actually sticking to their promises or telling the truth.

Spending referees exist to regulate public expenditure, and they do their jobs well. The National Audit Office (NAO) checks how public bodies have spent taxes, including that spending is well controlled and that there has been no fraud. Reports on poor expenditure go to Parliament's Public Accounts Committee for them to scrutinise. Around 39 countries also have regulators, like the Congressional Budget Office in the US or the Office for Budget Responsibility (OBR) in the UK, to provide independent analysis of public finances. The existence of these independent spending watchdogs acts as a check on those spending public money, but their reports necessarily take time to produce and can be technical to read, meaning report findings may be ignored.[9]

The Global Technological Revolution can now help us to do better and further improve the accountability of those spending public money, and help them to make spending decisions that align more closely with the wishes of the communities they lead. In our private lives, our personal online bank accounts enable us to see, whenever we want, how much money we have earned and how we have spent it. The creation of a personal online tax account could do the same for the public money that politicians take and spend, giving communities a clearer account of the taxation raised from them and how it was spent, as well as more control of their money and of the spending choices being made on their behalf.

Tax and spending

In 2016–17, the UK government raised about £717 billion in taxes, or about £13,500 for every adult.[10] This represents around 37 per cent of the UK's GDP. The money was raised in various ways. About 43 per cent came from taxes on income. These are deducted by employers from earnings at source or paid to the UK's tax authority, HMRC, following an assessment at the end of the year. Income tax rates tend to increase with earnings. In the US, there are seven income tax brackets, ranging from 10 per cent to 40 per cent, as well a basic level of untaxed income. Australia has five rates, including 0 per cent on incomes under AU$19,000 and 45 per cent on income earned over

AU$180,000. In the UK, in addition to four bands of income tax, from 0 per cent to 45 per cent, employees and employers must each pay a social security (National Insurance) tax of up to 13.8 per cent. Other income, including from gifts, bequests and interest payments, are also usually taxed.

About 4 per cent of public money in the UK is raised from property and other capital taxes, such as from the transfer of property, through inheritance or sale. In some countries, taxes also apply to other property, including boats and cars. Some argue that the UK has a £159 a year tax for owning a television[11] and up to £2,175 for owning a vehicle, depending on its engine size and level of carbon emissions.[12] These other levies and licence fees raise a further 5 per cent of overall income. In addition, most countries require residents to make an annual payment according to the estimated value of their property. In the UK, these council taxes bring in a further 4 per cent of overall government income. Collectively, these property and council taxes, levies and licence fees bring in 13 per cent of government income.

The UK raises a further 37 per cent of its income from taxes on goods and services, with 17 per cent coming from value-added tax (VAT), 10 per cent from taxes on companies and the remaining 10 per cent from taxes on, for example, fuel, alcohol and tobacco. A sales or 'value added' tax is applied in most countries to most purchases, with rates ranging up to 27 per cent in Hungary, 20 per cent in Monaco and the UK, to 12 per cent in the US. Some goods, including basic foods, are taxed at a lower rate, or not taxed at all. Other goods, including alcohol, petrol and tobacco, are taxed at higher rates. Sweden taxes online gambling at 18 per cent; Mexico imposes a 5 per cent tax on junk food; while Hungary, Ireland and France tax sugary drinks. In addition, businesses pay taxes on their profits at rates including 18 per cent in Switzerland, 25 per cent in Uruguay and 33.3 per cent in Monaco. These costs are passed on to customers in higher prices for goods and services.

There are other ways, beyond taxation, that communities raise money. People may be charged tuition fees at university, or pay for passports, medical prescriptions or other official services. There may be tolls to use roads, bridges or tunnels, parking fees at hospitals and colleges, charges for waste collection or entry to public museums, and fines for breaking rules such as for speeding or littering. Some businesses are publicly owned and also contribute funding. Collectively, the UK generates about 7 per cent of its public money from these sources.

Communities also borrow money. This must be paid for, just as we pay back loans when borrowing to buy a house or a car. The UK needed to borrow about £49 billion in 2016–17 on top of the taxes raised to fund its spending.[13] Borrowing by cities and countries provides money now, but it reduces the amount available to spend later, as loans are then paid back with interest.

The figures quoted here vary over time and will change significantly in the years after COVID-19 as governments, including in the UK, recover from the massive financial outlays and economic devastation. The figures vary markedly between countries. Income taxes, for example, tend to become a more significant source of funding as a country develops economically, with less developed countries taking more tax from businesses and from money transfers from abroad. Over 5 per cent of public money in Africa is received in development aid, with the sum exceeding 20 per cent in 2018 in the Central African Republic and Liberia.[14] Overall rates of taxation vary significantly too, from only 6 per cent in Afghanistan, to around 76 per cent in Albania. Across the 36 rich countries of the Organisation for Economic Co-operation and Development (OECD), the average that is taken in taxation is about 34 per cent, although it ranges from 25 per cent in Turkey, Chile and the US to 50 per cent in Denmark and Norway.[15]

This variation within and between countries, and over time, coupled with the multiple, complex ways that we are taxed, makes it difficult to know for sure how much of our money is taken in taxation, or how. But for the purposes here, we can assume as a rule of thumb that, as a UK resident, we may have around a third of our money taken in taxation each year in one way or another. So someone earning £40,000 might pay about £13,300 a year in tax, with perhaps half of this taken in income taxes and a third in VAT and other indirect taxes. This is a very rough calculation, with the exact amount dependent on the year in question, how the income is earned, the exact pattern of consumption, changes to government policy and much else. A good accountant could estimate our tax bill more precisely and help us to reduce it.

But matters become even more complicated when we consider not how taxes are raised, but rather how they are spent.

We often hear from politicians about how they want to spend public money. In the UK's 2017 General Election, for example, the Labour Party said that it would spend an extra £37 billion on the NHS in England. The Liberal Democrats, at the same election, said that it would give the NHS an extra £2 billion a year, while the Conservative Party said that its funding increases to the NHS would reach £8 billion extra a year by 2023. This all sounds good, but there is rarely enough context to make sense of such numbers. This allows for some exaggerated, misleading or contradictory claims. In this health example, for instance, it might be helpful to know that the 2017 UK health budget was about £122 billion a year and that, since 1948, the NHS has grown on average by 4 per cent a year above inflation, so an extra £7 billion a year in the health budget might be considered normal. But even then, it is a challenge to make sense of the promises being made or how they compare.

Figures and facts like these from politicians do not help us to answer the kind of basic questions that we have to answer when making decisions about our own household budget. In our everyday life, we know how much money comes into our home each month. If a person clears £1,000 a month in income, they may pay £450 on rent, £100 on utility bills, £250 on food and clothing and £150 on transport. That leaves £50 a month to cover entertainment, birthdays and holidays, as well as savings and emergencies. So, if they want new clothes for a wedding, for example, they may have to reduce spending elsewhere. And if they want a new car, they may need a loan and have to find an extra £50 a month to pay it back. And so on. These spending decisions are difficult. We cannot usually buy everything we want. And at times in our lives, the choices may be hard indeed: do we cut back on heating or on food?

Macroeconomics cannot simply be equated to household budgeting.[16] But some features of spending decisions made by a community are similar: an amount of money is available for spending, and there are more things to spend on than there is money for. So we need to make choices. Do we spend more on health, and if so, can we afford it? Must we cut back elsewhere, and if so, where? Can we pay for more police officers while also increasing the salaries of nurses and teachers? Do we upgrade our seaports or our submarines, if we cannot do both? And do we spend now, or save for the future?

Questions such as these are being asked and answered every week, locally and nationally, by politicians and those leading public services. Decisions are being made about how to spend taxes so that everyone benefits. But taxpayers are told little about these decisions – not only when they are being made, but afterwards too. Each government department and public body must, of course, publish their financial accounts each year, and the accounts are scrutinised by auditors. But accounts can be hard to understand, even for auditors. And most of us just aren't that interested. This makes it hard to piece together an overall picture of how our tax money is being spent on our behalf. Even the NAO, in its annual report on overall government expenditure, can only provide headlines because 'drilling down into further analysis has been challenging'.[17]

Instead, with the modern tools of technology and data analysis, it is becoming possible to present information far more clearly, so it is easier to understand where taxes are actually going. The UK think tank Demos is doing this by publishing an online Tax Calculator,[18] where anyone can make changes to a virtual tax system and see the impact of particular spending decisions. As another example of what should be possible, there is an analysis of the published accounts of UK government bodies from 2006–07 to show how spending information could be presented to taxpayers, with wide-ranging assumptions made to reduce duplication, avoid jargon and make the numbers add up.[19]

For every £1,000 that a UK taxpayer is taxed each year, money is broadly spent as follows:

- £315 is spent on welfare payments, including £58 on unemployment benefits, £56 on pensions, £66 on disability benefits and £129 on supporting families and those on low incomes.

- £126 is spent on education, including £37 on primary schools, £50 on secondary schools and £38 on universities and colleges.
- £119 is spent on health, including £41 on hospitals, £27 on medical research, £10 on social care and public health and £35 on staff salaries.
- £97 is spent on debt interest payments to banks and other creditors.
- £85 is spent on the armed forces, including £20 each to the Army, Navy and Air Force.
- £82 is spent on local issues, including £33 on housing and the remainder to local government projects.
- £60 is spent on administration, including £49 on tax collection and economic management, £8 on maintaining the country's legal system and £3 a year on running government and Parliament itself.
- £29 is spent to protect the environment, including £11 on agriculture and the countryside and £4 a year on food and animal health.
- £29 is spent on transport, including £11 on roads, £10 on the railways, £3 on shipping and £4 on aviation.
- £25 is spent on justice, including £7 on the police and other emergency services, £7 on prisons and £1.50 on the immigration system.
- £17 is spent overseas, including £4 in aid to Africa and £11 spent in Europe.
- £13 is spent on industry, including £3 on energy, £4 on science and technology and £2 on trade and exports.
- £3 is spent on the arts, sports, parks and tourism.

In other words, a UK taxpayer earning £40,000 a year, and paying about £13,300 in tax, would spend about £1,583 a year of their taxes on health services, £492 a year on primary schools, £146 on building and maintaining roads and so on. Economists and public sector auditors are welcome to correct these figures, as they are only accurate enough to give an idea of where tax money goes. Yet regardless of the accuracy of these particular figures, it is now technically possible for taxpayers to find out what they are. It is, after all, their money that is being spent.

UK taxpayers may be happy that pensions and welfare payments make up the biggest proportion of spending, almost three times more than is spent on health, and that more money is spent on repaying debt than on the armed forces. Or not. But knowing where their money goes may at least give them the option of trying to influence politicians to spend it more in line with the ways they want, as Demos is trying to encourage through its Tax Calculator. Voter influence tends to make politicians more responsive and accountable.

Transparent taxation in practice

There is already some visibility of the taxes we pay. Many receive a monthly payslip from their employers, or an annual tax statement, known in the UK as a P60.[20] Most shop receipts also show how much sales tax is paid as part of a purchase. And some local councils send annual statements to residents about the taxes raised in their communities, including to support the local police force.

But many taxes are invisible. We do not see the impact of corporation tax, for example, as we pay it indirectly. Perhaps future company receipts and invoices could estimate the amount of the transaction that is corporation tax, excises or tariffs, based on previous years. Thus, in 2014, Apple would have told its Irish customers that, VAT aside, just 50p of their new £1,000 laptop was being paid in tax, and Starbucks, from 2000 to 2014, would have told its British customers that it paid just 1p of tax from their £3 coffee. If companies are obliged to say, in each transaction, what percentage of their revenue they have given in tax to the local community, this may act as a reminder of their obligation to fund the legal and financial infrastructure that they depend on to do business.

With the technology now available, and with almost 80 per cent of purchases now being made electronically,[21] it may be possible to give taxpayers online access to the amount they have paid in tax, just as they can access their personal finances through an online bank account. A personal online tax account could track how much each person contributes to their community through all methods of taxation, whether in absolute terms or as a percentage of income. Data from employers and purchases could be combined to give a complete picture of the amount of money an individual contributes towards buying the collective benefits for their community that taxes pay for.

The online tax account might also show how taxes are being spent. Those spending public money could be responsible for producing an annual breakdown of the money that they have spent in a way that is easier to understand and accessible online. Taxpayers should not need the skills of an auditor or economist to have information about the choices made on their behalf with their own money.

Greater tax transparency has the potential to increase the accountability of decision-makers, reducing the Accountability Gap. It may also help build more realistic expectations of what it is possible for a community to do with public money, helping to close the Expectation Gap too.

We need many things for a community to work well, including clean streets, fresh air, the rule of law, health services and education. Taxes need to go a long way. If taxpayers can see more clearly what their money must pay for, including the massive costs of unexpected crises such as COVID-19, and how their money must pay for long-term investment as well as meeting today's needs, then they may better appreciate that public services cannot arrive like an internet delivery from Amazon. In our private lives, we can spend more money on something and expect a better product or service, because we know that buying cheap may mean compromising on quality. Greater tax transparency would make it clearer that this also applies to public spending. Seeing the cost of public services can help us to judge whether we are getting good value for money or not.

Greater tax transparency would put governments under more scrutiny to spend money well. Waste and corruption would be easier to identify if better published information enables comparisons in spending between different places. It could reduce the complexity of the tax system too, encouraging governments to set taxes that are easier to understand and to comply with. Simpler, predictable taxes that cost less to administer raise more money for public services.[22] This, in turn, can reduce tax avoidance. Tax exemptions and loopholes will become more visible, creating pressure for them to be closed. Greater transparency may also create pressure on us to pay tax if we become more aware that tax avoidance is not a victimless crime against an anonymous state with no losers.

Greater tax transparency internationally could enable a future world parliament to limit the ability of global companies to avoid taxes. Instead of being able to move money from one tax jurisdiction to another, big tech firms, global banks, pharmaceutical and other multinational companies would have to pay taxes on their global earnings to a single accountable authority, with the money returned to communities in benefits such as improved environmental protection, clearer trade rules and less cyber-crime.

Knowing more about our taxes might even make us happier, strange as this may seem. UK taxpayers like paying National Insurance more than income tax because we mistakenly believe that it is ring-fenced to specific, tangible benefits.[23] Similarly, patients with access to their detailed health records not only have a better understanding of their condition and are therefore less anxious, but also have fewer questions for their doctors, thus saving money. Their treatments are also more likely to be successful.[24] No one has a greater interest in our own health than ourselves. We should also have access to the same amount of information about our money.

Implementing a new rule of democracy

Gathering accurate information about tax spending and presenting it to each taxpayer individually and comprehensibly online would be complicated and expensive. Governments may think it not worth the bother, even though mobile phone, finance and retail firms all consider it worthwhile to gather enormous quantities of data about their customers' spending every hour of every day. The technology exists for us to find out and display how our taxes are taken and where they are spent.

Many of us may not be interested in looking at a personal online tax account or in seeing how our taxes have been taken or spent. Most of us do not even look at our monthly bank statements. This is because we generally trust our bank to keep our money safe. If we similarly trust politicians and public bodies to spend public money wisely, and we trust the regulatory referees of democracy such as the NAO to examine public spending and challenge waste on our behalf, then we may not need to look at our online tax account either. It would be costly information to provide if there is no tangible benefit. But having access to this personal information about our taxes is an option that, in future, we might want to have available.

Without it, we may be less able to influence politicians to spend our money in line with our wishes and we might see value in a new rule of democracy that 'how taxes are raised and spent should be wholly transparent to those paying the taxes, with sufficient tax-raising powers at every democratic level where politicians make spending decisions on behalf of their communities'.

Taxation need not be a game of hide and seek, where we try to find out how our money is taken; nor public spending a game of poker, where we can only guess how it is being spent. Instead, tax and spending might be considered a jigsaw, with bits of money from lots of places having to fund multiple public services. It is not an easy jigsaw to put together, but if all the pieces are on display, then members of a community can at least work to fit them together in the best possible way. At the moment, the pieces are not even on the table.

Politicians and public servants must be able to use their professional judgement and their understanding of complex issues to make choices about how best to spend public funds. That is the point of representative democracy and what makes it effective. We elect people to make decisions for us, so we do not have to. Individual taxpayers should not have the final say over how taxes are raised or spent.

But nor is it right that public money is spent without public scrutiny, so taxpayers are unable to see how the game of democracy is played, or whether it is being played well. Today's tools of technology and real-time data analysis can provide better ways to show where public money has gone. The same technology can help taxpayers to express spending preferences and contribute to a more informed debate about the relative costs and benefits of spending public money in particular ways.

Implementing a new rule of democracy along these lines to make taxation more transparent would help to make politics more accountable, support the work of existing spending regulators, including the NAO and OBR in the UK, and help to close the Accountability Gap that has grown as a result of the Global Technological Revolution.

The rules for politicians

We want politicians to obey the law, and to play by the rules of democracy too. These rules hold politicians to account: we can take them to court if we think they have broken the law, and if we don't like the decisions they have made on our behalf, we can vote them out of power.

The Global Technological Revolution has weakened the effectiveness of the existing rules of democracy as they apply to politicians. The rules need to become more responsive to reflect a faster-moving world. The internet has created new ways for a few politicians to evade the rules. And, because the Global Technological Revolution has created more complex, interconnected communities with higher expectations of public services, it has become more difficult to work out what politicians have actually achieved, and to hold them to account. It may be time for new ways to assure ourselves that politicians are acting in our interests, and a new rule of democracy:

Politicians must adhere to the rule of law and the rules of democracy, including by being accountable for their words, their actions and the impact of their decisions.

The existing rules of democracy for politicians

At the heart of the rules of democracy is the ability they give us periodically to elect someone from among competing candidates to represent us when decisions are made about our community. It is a powerful way to hold those with power to account. If politicians want our support, they must try to understand and respond to our wishes and achieve results, or we can reject them.

Politicians therefore take elections very seriously, however self-confident or even arrogant they may seem. Their job is on the line. And if their job goes, so may their income, their prestige and their standing in the community. Few defeated politicians return to public life, and some struggle to find work. Employers can be reluctant to take on ex-MPs, perhaps because of their political views or because they have few up-to-date professional skills. Some former politicians, partly as a result of short-term financial hardship and their abrupt change of social status, can lose self-esteem and become clinically depressed.[1]

Politicians often know their tenure is fragile and may be short. They see political friends unexpectedly lose elections through no fault of their own, due to wider social changes or mistakes by party leaders. Election results can sweep aside long-serving politicians. Labour MPs were elected across Scotland for decades until 2015, when the Scottish National Party won 56 of 59 constituencies. In France in 2017, 379 Socialist and Republican politicians lost their jobs as voters turned to Emmanuel Macron's new political party, La République en Marche! Defeated politicians might bemoan the capricious nature of democracy. But it is its great strength. It makes political decision-makers accountable to those they represent.

But this great strength of democracy also makes the stakes at election time extremely high for politicians themselves. The result will lead to power or oblivion. Many in the UK remember the moment in 1997 when Michael Portillo, once tipped as a future Conservative prime minister, was rejected by his North London voters, or in 2015, when Ed Balls, for many years at the heart of the Labour government, lost his job as an MP in West Yorkshire. Both subsequently found work in television. Both would have preferred power.

Because the stakes are so high, the temptation is also high for a few politicians to cheat to reduce the risk of election loss.[2] Rather than play fairly by the rules of democracy, they try to undermine both the rules and the referees, so that they can win.

Historically, they may have tried, for example, to manipulate the boundaries of electoral communities. This 'gerrymandering'[3] enables politicians to rig elections by choosing their voters rather than have the voters choose them. As one example from many in the US, the shape of the fourth congressional district in Illinois is no natural community. It resembles giant crab claws joined at a base 12 miles away. Yet it keeps all the Hispanic voters in one place. Many countries, including the UK, have eliminated this risk by establishing independent Boundary Commissions to enforce fair rules when constituencies are defined. The Boundary Commissions for England, Scotland and Wales were established in 1944 to advise on the fair distribution of parliamentary constituencies. All are led by High Court judges.

Some politicians cheat by trying to buy votes. This happens crudely with free gifts to voters, including cash and alcohol, as has happened in India, Brazil, Nigeria and elsewhere. As recently as October 2019 a Japanese politician, Isshu Sugawara, resigned for bribing his voters with melons, oranges and fish roe. But buying votes also happens indirectly when politicians spend large sums on advertising, campaign workers, rallies and endorsements. This puts rich politicians and political parties at an advantage, and more accountable to their donors than to their voters. Most democracies recognise this risk. Independent Electoral Commissions act as referees of democracy during votes, enforcing spending rules, with sanctions including imprisonment for those who exceed established limits. The New Zealand Electoral Commission found that over NZ$1 million was illegally spent during the 2005 election, leading to political resignations and financial repayments. The Election Commission of India has been enforcing campaign finance law since 1950, after its independence was written into the Indian constitution.[4]

A few politicians have even tried outright electoral fraud. This has involved manipulating the voting register to prevent opponents from voting, or imposing bureaucratic hurdles to reduce turnout, such as by making voters present a certain document or vote at a specific time or place. Texas, for example, accepts a gun permit as proof of identity but not a student card.[5] Unscrupulous politicians may also try to coerce voters to allow someone else to vote for them, or intimidate or threaten voters with violence, or create ballot papers that confuse voters, or stop opposition candidates standing for election at all, or bribe election officials not to count votes. Such practices are rightly suspected when the president of Turkmenistan won 97 per cent of the national vote in 2013, or the Uzbek president won 91 per cent of the votes cast in 2007. There are other recent examples from Belarus to Uganda.

For the game of democracy to be a success, so that we are all equally represented when decisions about our community are made, the rules of democracy must not only be fair, but also be applied consistently and independently. Indeed, the rules of democracy have evolved over time to make sure this is the case. In 1856, South Australia introduced electoral registers and secret ballots, rather than rely on a public show of hands, to reduce fraud and coercion. The innovation spread and is now accepted as a crucial part of the rules of democracy. Other rules require elections to be organised independently and run by officials who are not bullied by those with power or money. There are usually penalties for those who break the rules, however important the rule-breakers think they are. In many cases, elections are monitored by independent observers, such as by officials from another country or from a non-governmental organisation, to try to ensure politicians play by the rules.

In these ways, free, fair elections allow a range of candidates to display their views to us. We can then elect the candidate we most want to represent us when decisions are made about our communities. Once politicians have been elected, other referees ensure that they play by the rules too. In the UK, these include the Independent Parliamentary Standards Authority (IPSA), which sets the salaries and pensions of MPs and gives them a budget to employ staff and rent an office to do their jobs, and the Parliamentary Commissioner for Standards, who investigates allegations that MPs have broken Parliament's behavioural code of conduct.

These existing referees of the rules of democracy – Boundary Commissions, Electoral Commissions and Standards Authorities – ensure fairness when we ask politicians to represent us. Like all referees, their work is often unseen by the voters who watch the game of democracy. And, also like referees, these democratic regulators are usually unpopular with the politicians being refereed. The effectiveness and independence of these regulators of democracy can be improved, but they exist both to be fair to politicians who are doing their best, and to safeguard the rules against cheating, on behalf of the public. Both the Electoral Commission and IPSA, albeit rarely, have referred politicians to the police for potential misconduct.[6] Without democratic regulators such as these, as in any game without a referee, foul play risks being unchecked.

These referees of democracy are needed so that the game of democratic decision-making is played fairly and for our benefit. But in the wake of the Global Technological Revolution, we may need additional referees to ensure fair play. This is because it has become more possible for politicians to lie to win power. Or, if they do not lie, they misrepresent the truth, or promise success, or indeed say anything they want to win votes. And there are currently few rules of democracy that allow us to call them to account for their words.

Cynics may say that 'politics' and 'lies' are two sides of the same coin, and that the concepts live together like roses and thorns. It is true that many politicians change their views over time, and that they can make contradictory statements to different people. And some politicians have always lied rather than uphold the seven Nolan Principles of public life, including honesty.[7] But before the Global Technological Revolution, the words of politicians tended to be mediated by newspaper or TV editors who could be taken to court when they published anything defamatory or untrue. Now, through the internet and social media, politicians have unmediated instant contact with millions of voters. A few of them say whatever they like with few or no consequences. Twitter and Facebook cannot currently be prosecuted for comments made on their platforms.[8]

As such, a few politicians can spread false information or insult their political opponents to promote division and anger. Or they may lie about their own past. Donald Trump claimed that he had paid all his taxes, that Barack Obama had been born in Kenya, and that the 2020 presidential election had been stolen. In this way, such politicians may gain widespread coverage for their comments, particularly in social media. They hope that this will translate into financial and political support.

Few politicians lie outright. But politicians have always made promises. Some of these have been broken. In 2008 Barack Obama promised to reform healthcare and the criminal justice system, to cut taxes and close the detention centre in Guantanamo Bay. Some promises he fulfilled; some he did not. In 2016, many UK citizens thought they were being promised a £350 million a week dividend for the NHS if they voted to leave the EU. Regardless of the reasons for such failures to deliver, if someone has voted on the basis of a specific promise, they may risk feeling let down by politicians, and by democracy, if the promise is not then delivered.

At the moment, however, there are few incentives for politicians not to lie or to make unmeetable promises. They may calculate that people will forget their lies or promises, or at least have no way to hold them to account for them. And if one politician achieves success by lying and promising the earth, and by not playing fairly by the rules, then other politicians, however honourable, may be tempted to do the same. This risks a downward spiral where politicians with intelligence and integrity are defeated, and we are left with only chancers and cheaters in power.

This cannot be right. As children, we are taught to tell the truth. As adults, we are bound legally to tell the truth if called to testify in court. We could be imprisoned if we do not. A business cannot tell its customers that its face cream will make them live longer, or that this new car is good for the environment, or that investing in its fund will earn them millions, unless these statements are true. In the UK, the Advertising Standards Authority says that businesses 'must hold documentary evidence to prove all claims, whether direct or implied, that are capable of objective substantiation', and that claims made by businesses should not 'mislead or be likely to mislead, by inaccuracy, ambiguity, exaggeration, omission or otherwise'.[9] The Federal Trade Commission in the US has a similar role. In 2005 the EU passed a law on unfair commercial practices that prohibits 23 ways of misleading consumers, including giving false information or omitting important information when making a sale.[10] Companies that do not comply can be taken to court, prosecuted and fined. Rogue firms can be closed down.

It may now be necessary to update the rules of democracy in parallel with these rules for business. Just as commercial firms must make accurate promises if they want customers' money, it may be time for political candidates to do the same if they want their electorate's vote. If businesses cannot lie about their competitors with impunity, politicians should not be able to make things up, or make unfounded personal attacks on their opponents. Promises should not be thrown cheaply at voters, as if they have no meaning. Rather, their words must matter and have consequences. By all means they can promise that, if elected, they will close a detention centre or build a wall. And they can say that their opponent is mad or bad. But perhaps, like business and us, politicians should also know that, if they don't do what they say, or if they are found to have knowingly lied or slandered their opponents, they can be held to account.

Holding politicians to account for their words

Holding politicians to account for what they say can, of course, be done by ejecting them from office at the next election. But to hold politicians to account for their words in more detail may involve strengthening the rules of democracy. This would be difficult, but it could be done.

In many countries, it is illegal to lie under oath in court. This is known as 'perjury'. It is also illegal to knowingly make a false, fictitious or fraudulent statement in administering public affairs, even when not in court. This is called 'misconduct in public office'. It is also illegal to tell lies that harm another's reputation, with laws to prohibit defamation, libel and slander.[11] In the UK, hate speech is also illegal, including any communication that is threatening or abusive, and is intended to harass, alarm or distress someone.[12] But convictions in these areas can be hard to secure. This is partly because, in the US, for example, to convict someone of defamation, you must prove that a person has (a) made a false statement; (b) done so without adequate research into its truthfulness; and (c) caused harm by doing so. The courts, when deciding whether someone has told a lie or not, place the burden of proof on the person challenging the untrue statement rather than on the person making it. This is for the good reason that a defendant is presumed innocent until proved guilty. So the prosecution needs to prove beyond reasonable doubt both that a politician lied and that they intended to lie.

This emphasis may need to change. The law could instead ensure that candidates for election are more incentivised to tell the truth. The legal burden of proof could shift to politicians so that, if challenged, they would need to convince a court that: (a) they made a true statement; (b) that they did so with adequate research into its truthfulness; and (c) that no harm was caused by doing so. As with advertising assertions by businesses, the burden might need to be on the speaker to account for the truth of their words, not on the listener to prove them a liar. Politics will never be polite. The stakes are simply too high. And politicians win our votes partly by persuading us with words. This may involve criticising their opponent, including by using banter or repartee to get a laugh, but when banter becomes defamation, and when arguments are won with lies, then the law may need to change so politicians are held to account for what they say.

There are already courts in place to do this. Election Courts hear petitions against the result of an election to settle disputes and alleged irregularities. They have existed in the UK since 1868, when the Parliamentary Elections Act took the power to adjudicate election disputes away from Parliament itself. In 2010, a defeated politician in Oldham, Elwyn Watkins, argued that the result of the election had been affected by false statements made during the campaign by the winner, Phil Woolas. The Election Court found Mr Woolas guilty, banned him from elected office for three years, and ordered a rerun of the election. In 2015 the Election Court removed Lutfur Rahman from office as mayor of Bethnal Green in East London after finding him to be personally guilty of 'corrupt or illegal practices, or both'. The election was rerun and Mr Rahman was prohibited from standing for elected office again until 2021.[13]

Election Courts already have the power to remove politicians from office, order reruns of elections and prevent corrupt or illegal candidates from standing again. If they were used more frequently, particularly with strengthened laws, politicians may become more conscious that they will need to defend their words and explain why their statements were true, or why they believed them to be true, and be held to account for any insults that caused harm to others, including their opponents, so that elections are not won under false pretences or by not playing by the rules of democracy. Politicians who lie could be challenged after an election, and be removed or banned from office if found guilty, so that they play by the rules.

However, unlike lies and insults, which are assertions that relate to current or past circumstances, and which can be tested in court, promises relate to the future. So, while an Election Court may determine whether a political statement at election time is true or untrue, or has caused harm or not, no court can know, at the time of an election, or until many years afterwards, whether a promise made to win votes will be met or not. It may nonetheless be possible for politicians to be held to account for them.

Politicians do not need to make promises to win our votes. When a selection panel interviews a candidate for a job, it looks at their background and their experience, and listens to what they have to say, including under pressure. As voters, we can similarly assess which candidate most shares our values and aspirations for our community. Candidates talk about their past and why they've done what they've done. They talk about their beliefs and what matters to them. They describe their vision for the future too.

A politician's background, experience, vision and their composure under pressure are all good reasons to decide who to vote for. We are electing someone we must trust to make the right decisions on our behalf in unknowable future situations. We do not need their specific promises to make this choice. Indeed, a panel interviewing candidates for a job looks for experience and potential, not a promise or guarantee of success.

It may be time to consider the value of a political promise more explicitly. A promise is a specific offer, made in an election campaign in return for a vote. Businesses, when advertising their products, must prove all claims 'that are capable of objective substantiation'. Candidates for election might also be required to fulfil all campaign promises that are capable of objective measurement. They might similarly be prohibited from misleading voters by 'inaccuracy, ambiguity, exaggeration or omission'.[14]

Thus, if a candidate describes their *vision* for a community as one with lower taxes and improved education, then that, alongside other factors, may be enough for voters to elect them. But if they specifically *promise* that they will cut basic income tax to 20 per cent, and make sure that all children can read and write by age 11, then they should know that they will be held to account if the promises are not kept.

Promises could be independently verified. Just as the Electoral Commission and Boundary Commissions independently determine whether elections are conducted fairly, and the OBR offers independent views on the government's financial statements, so a 'Promises Commission' could independently assess whether politicians' campaign promises have been met or not. A watchdog along these lines might determine what promises had been made by whom, and periodically draw on evidence to assess which had been met. And, like any regulator, it might need to impose sanctions on failing to meet careless promises beyond the risk of losing a distant election.

Political promises vary. Some, such as to keep a library open, may be easier to achieve. Others, like a promise to improve healthcare, are more difficult. The consequences of failure also differ. And there may be mitigating reasons for broken promises, including unexpected events, such as a factory closure or a global pandemic. Yet even unexpected events should not prevent voters from having an opportunity to check, between elections, whether politicians have made good on their promises, or at least tried to, in good faith. This is normal in other walks of life. If we are given a four-year work contract, we know that our contract may not be renewed when it ends, particularly if things don't go well. But in the interim, we also have performance reviews. These regular checks help us to find out if our work is on track. We can make adjustments if it is not. Mid-term reviews might help improve politicians' performance too.

Politicians are already much scrutinised. They are challenged by the media, by other politicians and in town hall meetings in their own constituency. But there is no formal mechanism by which they are accountable to those they represent, between elections, for their words and promises. Like other workers, politicians could have performance reviews with their bosses, the electorate, including on whether they and their political parties were meeting their election promises. The format of the reviews might vary from place to place. They may include citizens' assemblies or other mechanisms of deliberative democracy,[15] as well as older-style reports or meetings. But some way to scrutinise politicians between elections could help to respond to the speed of change taking place in modern communities as a result of the Global Technological Revolution. An independent Promises Commission, and a formal mid-term review process, might allow voters to take action if a politician has lied or broken promises.

The action should be democratic too. If a politician has lied, misled others, broken their promises or behaved badly or illegally, they should be held to account by asking again the basic question at the heart of the rules of democracy: do we still want this person to represent us and our interests, or not?

Recalling politicians from a parliament or council to stand again for election is a means of accountability used in many countries. People in the Philippines can recall politicians when 25 per cent of a community formally requests it. In Colombia, the proportion is 30 per cent. Politicians in the US can also be recalled – recalls were introduced in Los Angeles in 1903 and in Oregon in 1908 to inhibit 'misconduct or incompetence while in office'. There were 150 recall elections in 17 states in 2011, with 75 of these votes ending the term of the politician concerned. The recall mechanism was put into UK law in 2015 and was used once in 2018 and twice in 2019, removing two MPs from office, one for lying and the other for fraud.[16] A mid-term review process could give communities an opportunity to trigger a recall vote if sufficient people have lost confidence in the way they are represented, as long as the proportion of voters needed to ask for a recall is sufficiently high to prevent permanent elections.

Being held to account for their words by democratic regulators, such as Electoral Commissions, Election Courts, a Promises Commission, and ultimately, by voters, at the risk of losing their job, might help politicians to think more carefully about what they say to win votes. It could help them to play more fairly by the rules of democracy. The vast majority of politicians work hard to play by the rules of the game – they behave with integrity in often challenging circumstances, and they are as honest as the rest of us. But they may be inclined to make more realistic promises and tell fewer lies if they can be held more strongly to account.

This could help to close the Expectation Gap between what we are led to believe is possible and what can actually be done to improve public services and other aspects of community life.

Holding politicians to account for their decisions

It is not enough just to hold politicians to account for what they *say*, but also for what they *do*. This applies to a particular subset of politicians. While all politicians can debate issues of importance on our behalf and can vote on legislation, those few politicians who temporarily hold executive power also get to decide what to do about these issues, and can propose new laws and other changes to the rules that govern our lives.

These executive politicians include prime ministers, mayors and council leaders. Others have specific executive responsibilities, such as for defence or education or social care, as a government minister or local councillor. This subset of executive politicians acts not only on behalf of their own voters, but of everyone. This means they should listen to the views of everyone, and then decide what is in the best interests of the whole community, not just their own voters. These politicians are decision-makers as well as representatives; they govern as well as campaign. With their greater responsibility comes greater accountability.

The rules of democracy already allow for these executive politicians to be held to account for their decisions by other politicians in opposition to the government. Their role is to hold decision-makers to account on behalf of all voters. They debate and challenge executive decisions in detail precisely so we do not have to do this ourselves on issue after issue, whether a change to fishing licences or a new science curriculum. This is representative democracy in action.

In general, politicians hold each other to account well. They challenge decision-makers both in Parliament and outside it. A particularly effective way for them to do this is through the committees of politicians set up specifically to scrutinise legislation, public bodies and ministers, and hold decision-makers to account. In the UK, the present system of Select Committees was developed in 1979 from earlier, weaker arrangements to scrutinise government departments and agencies and to hold ministers to account for their decisions. They have been broadly effective, particularly in exposing new evidence, and around 40 per cent of their recommendations to government have been accepted.[17] At times, their impact is more dramatic. In April 2018, Home Secretary Amber Rudd was forced to resign after misleading the Home Affairs Select Committee about targets to remove illegal immigrants.[18]

Politicians hold each other to account in other ways, including by issuing calls for action on particular issues or requesting public inquiries to examine why things went badly wrong. In extreme cases, politicians can try to prosecute decision-makers and remove them from office. In Ireland, India, the Philippines, Russia, the US and elsewhere, elected politicians can be impeached if they have committed crimes or serious abuses of their office. Brazilian President Dilma Rousseff and South Korean President Park Geun-hye were both impeached in 2016. In some parliamentary systems, a vote of no confidence can similarly lead to the resignation of decision-makers and potentially an election and a change of government. The prime minister of Spain was ousted in this way in 2018.[19]

Votes of no confidence and impeachment are rare because they are rightly hard to achieve. Political decision-makers in executive roles should not be in daily fear of losing their jobs, yet they should also know that, just like anyone else doing a job, they will be regularly held to account for their performance and, if things go badly wrong, they will be ejected from office. Scrutiny by other politicians is effective in doing this.

But scrutiny can be improved. Sometimes members of Select Committees are reluctant to ask tough questions of politicians from their own party. And some are more interested in raising their own profile than in holding others to account, or give a speech rather than ask a question. Some committee members may simply be ill prepared or inadequately briefed.[20] This might be improved if Select Committees are more focused in their work planning, think about longer term improvements as well as tomorrow's headlines, collaborate with each other, and publish an annual report on their committee's work that reviews and assesses their success in holding decision-makers to account.

More importantly, Select Committees need better support. In the UK, committees generally rely on a team of up to six parliamentary staff to prepare papers and call witnesses. Politicians on the committee often conduct their own research, or rely on briefings from lobby groups, to know where to probe and what questions to ask. In local government, scrutiny committees can be completely unfunded, and rely on support from the same staff who support the executive politicians, creating conflicts of interest. In contrast, the congressional committees in the US have around 50 staff each.

In the UK, Parliament's Public Accounts Committee should be the model to follow. It has the support of the 800 staff at the NAO, the UK's public spending referee, to supply it with analysis on where taxpayers' money may have been misspent. All other Select Committees could have similar access to the expertise of the independent regulators and inspectorates that already scrutinise public services and other decision-making. The chief inspector of prisons could have a reporting line to the Justice Select Committee, and Ofsted, the inspectorate of schools and colleges, to the Education Select Committee. As the referees of public services, these regulators and inspectorates are responsible for reporting honestly on the quality of services and for upholding the rules and laws agreed by our politicians in Parliament. It is harder for these referees to play that fair, independent role if they are part of government themselves, inspecting their own paymaster. Regulators and inspectorates should instead be more accountable to a democratic parliament that holds executive decision-makers to account.

Select Committees could also hold a wider range of politicians to account, including those who have left office. The tenure of decision-makers is usually much shorter than the impact of their decisions. UK government ministers are in the same job on average for 28 months, after which they are shuffled to new responsibilities or leave government altogether: the Ministry of Defence had three different secretaries of state – Liam Fox, Philip Hammond and Michael Fallon – between May 2010 and July 2014. Two years in a role is generally enough for someone to get to know a job and its challenges, and to make some decisions, but not long enough to see through any significant changes, especially if the politician is responsible for complex issues and public services. Only after time can we know whether decisions were wise or foolish. A government minister can cut funding for foreign language teaching or change waste management regulations, but they are unlikely to be around to deal with any resulting lack of interpreters or increased pollution.

The short tenure of decision–makers, and the knowledge that they will not personally be held to account for their decisions, is bound to influence their behaviour. However much they have the overall interests of their community at heart, they may prioritise shorter term over longer term considerations, giving greater weight to next week's parliamentary debate than to the needs of the next generation or to long-term value for money. This risks poorer decisions and politicians prioritising their survival over the needs of the people they represent.

A case study might be Chris Grayling MP. In 2013, he was the UK's justice minister. He cut funding for probation services and privatised them, despite widespread warnings that the rapid, sweeping changes would be risky. Contrary to Mr Grayling's promises, the reforms did not reduce reoffending and failed to increase efficiency.[21] In 2019 the policy was reversed. Mr Grayling's decision to restrict books in prison was also overturned by his successor. But he had then moved to be responsible for transport, and there was no way for him to be held to account for his previous poor decisions.

This gap in accountability can be addressed. It should be routine for executive politicians like Mr Grayling to be held to account by parliamentary Select Committees, even after they have left office. Knowing that they could be held to account for their decisions in the future may impact on how politicians make decisions now. They will still consider short-term factors, including the immediate media reaction, but may be more likely to consider the longer term impact of decisions if they could be examined by a Select Committee in 10 years' time. Decision-makers would have qualified immunity, so they are protected from prosecution if they make reasonable decisions in good faith while following proper processes.[22] But acts of illegality and gross incompetence could be challenged. And better scrutiny of decisions could lead to more balanced and effective decision-making, and some failures avoided. Unless our elected representatives can hold decision-makers to account, politicians have the power to take decisions they will not be accountable for, however badly the decisions turn out.

Accountable politicians

The problems of political lies, insults, broken promises and poor decision-making are far from new. Yet they have been amplified by the pervasive internet megaphones created by the Global Technological Revolution and have created new challenges for democracy. These problems can be addressed. The solutions proposed here are legal and institutional. They are unlikely to prevent late-night lies and insults on social media.

But the law and the creation of institutions are the ways that, over centuries, the rules of democracy have evolved and grown stronger. This slow evolution is better than inaction and having to accept that politicians will forever meet lie with lie, promise with promise, and insult with insult. Since the establishment of the Cortes of León in 1188 and the acceptance of the Magna Carta in 1215,[23] communities have constrained the powerful through the law and through institutions. Little by little, the lawlessness of the powerful to do what they please has been eroded with a new law here, a new regulation there, and agreed institutional constraints. This process is described in the rules of democracy summarised in Chapter 1, where 'decisions ... become codified into rules. ... People ... are required to adhere to these rules on penalty of enforceable sanctions. The laws and accepted practice change over time' and where politicians 'establish institutions ... in line with their decisions and the rules they have created'.

Bureaucracy may be slow, and justice takes time. This is because the law must be fair. This also means being fair to politicians. They should not lie or make promises that really can't be met. But they should also be allowed to campaign vigorously for votes, and to set out their competing visions for their community and explain strongly, but honestly, where they disagree with others.

The rules of democracy, and institutions such as Electoral Commissions and Boundary Commissions, exist to make the decision-making processes for our community fairer. That steady fairness of the law and of institutions, independently refereed by the courts and regulators, is an effective way to hold politicians to account for their words and deeds. Politicians are already constrained by the law. Due to the Equality Act 2010, they cannot make decisions that discriminate against those with protected characteristics, including disability, race and religion. The information they use to make decisions is disclosable under the Freedom of Information Act 2000. And the National Audit Act 1983 makes all their decisions subject to independent audit and scrutiny by Parliament.

These laws do not stop executive politicians from making difficult decisions. But they do add constraints and increase the stakes in what is already a hard job. Improving the accountability of politicians through the law will add pressure on them to do the right thing, not just for tomorrow, but for the longer term. It is because the stakes are so high that their decision-making should not to be subject to random personal prejudice, but be constrained by agreed rules to help them make the best decisions they can.

Evolving the rules of democracy so that politicians are more accountable may lead to more boring politics: fewer lies and insults, fewer exciting promises, and decision-making that gives greater weight to longer term considerations. Politics will still be unpredictable, although politicians may be less entertaining. But, in choosing someone to represent us when difficult decisions are made about our communities, we are not picking a film star or game show host. We are electing someone to represent our interests and to do their best when our community faces complex unknown future challenges, such as those brought about by COVID-19, globalisation or a technological revolution. And we then simply ask them to be accountable to us for their decisions, as in a new rule of democracy, where 'Politicians must adhere to the rule of law and the rules of democracy, including by being accountable for their words, their actions and the impact of their decisions'.

A public service guarantee

Politicians' greater accountability may lead to fewer, more selective political promises that are more likely to be met. In future, even more evidence-based ways to compare commitments from different politicians may be possible. For example, it may reduce the confusion of competing political promises if communities could establish an agreed baseline for the level of public services that they expect to receive in return for their taxes. This baseline could form a minimum public service guarantee.

A public service guarantee might define the minimum or basic level of expected public service performance. It might mean a guaranteed number of doctors for every 1,000 people. The average across the OECD in 2017 was 3.0, with 2.8 doctors per 1,000 people in the UK. Austria, Germany, Italy, Lithuania, Norway and Switzerland all have more than 4 doctors for every 1,000 people.[24] There could be similar guaranteed minimums in other areas of public services. Whatever minimum levels are set, they would be guaranteed, perhaps with a tax refund when expected minimum standards of education, health and transportation are not met.

Such guarantees may help voters to compare election offers from different politicians, and to vote for those who prioritise what they value most. Alongside a personal online tax account, a public service guarantee might give voters more complete information about how public money is being spent on their behalf. Our online tax account would tell us what tax we have paid, and the public service guarantee would tell us what minimum guaranteed standards of service to expect in return.

A formal public service guarantee along these lines is hard to envisage, although the UN is producing ideas to balance responsibilities to pay tax with rights to minimum standards.[25] Yet it may be one response to the current position where politicians are elected on the basis of vague or unevidenced promises.

When we spend our own money and buy a product or service from a commercial firm, we expect the goods to be as advertised. We have legal recourse to financial compensation if they are not. The same approach may need to be adopted in future for tax-funded public services. When we vote for a politician to participate in decision-making on our behalf, we enter into an implicit agreement. We elect them and give them the authority to make decisions for us, including the right to tax us; in return, we might come to expect certain, clearly defined benefits for us and for our community. As a consumer, we have the right to receive the products and services we pay for, or to get a refund if we don't. We might expect the same rights as a taxpayer. In both cases, we are spending our own money in order to receive something that we should have a right to expect.

In this way, setting guaranteed performance levels for public services might increase the accountability of elected politicians, helping to close the Accountability Gap between them and us that currently exists. It may also help to close the Expectation Gap, by making it clearer that the standards that we can expect from public services will not be the same as those we expect from Amazon or Google.

Clearer expectations of public services may not be easy to accept if we are guaranteed only minimum standards, but it might at least provide us with a specific, concrete way to hold politicians to account for their work, and help us to be more realistic about what is possible to do with the taxes we pay.

New rules and greater accountability

The proposals in this book to change the rules of democracy, including with a global parliament, a personal online tax account, guaranteed levels of public services, and new laws and institutions to hold politicians to account, may now be unrealistic. They are untested suggestions. They also involve asking politicians, who have spent years working to achieve influence, to give it away to others and to constrain themselves with new laws and new institutions. This is like asking tigers, roaming free and eating at will, to volunteer to live in an enclosure fenced off from livestock.

Yet the proposals are suggested as a response to the challenges created by the Global Technological Revolution and the concern that those making decisions about communities are unaccountable, and unable to meet the rising expectations of public services. The proposals aim to strengthen confidence that politicians are working on behalf of their voters, and to give us greater influence, albeit not control, over the decisions that affect our lives. New rules of democracy might help politicians to play the game of decision-making better on our behalf.

Democracy has evolved before. It was once thought preposterous for the working classes or for women to vote or stand for election, or for those born enslaved to have equal rights, or for politicians to be open about their sexuality, or for alleged war criminals to stand trial. None of these changes was easy.

In future, new rules of democracy could ensure a fairer contest between candidates for votes, and politicians who are more accountable once elected. This might not only help them to make better decisions, but also give us greater confidence in the effectiveness of democracy itself.

6

The rules for public services

Strengthening the rules of democracy for politicians might help to narrow a widening Accountability Gap between decision-makers and us, but stronger political accountability will not, on its own, improve financially stretched public services that face ever-increasing demands.

The rules of democracy may also need to evolve to ensure that public services, and the 5.3 million people in the UK who work in them as teachers, care workers, nurses, police officers and many others, are able to respond to the new demands created by the Global Technological Revolution. Otherwise, the Expectation Gap, between the public services we expect and what we actually receive, may continue to grow. A new rule of democracy could be as follows:

All organisations receiving taxes must be accountable both for how they spend public money and for sharing their learning and good practice.

The Global Technological Revolution has raised expectations of public services, and changed the needs of local communities, faster than public services have been able to respond. Public services are also now provided in more complex ways than before, including by businesses and charities as well as by public sector bodies, sometimes leading to unclear responsibilities. Public services can respond more effectively to these demands and challenges through stronger rules of democratic accountability.

The existing rules of democratic accountability

According to the current rules of democracy, politicians set up public bodies in order to improve life in communities in specific ways. These bodies are then accountable to politicians for their work and their spending.

Most public bodies already have a strong culture of playing by the rules, including the rule of law and the rules of democracy. Public sector workers know that they must act within the law and spend taxpayers' money carefully. These are core public service values. Public sector workers usually also have a strong sense of personal responsibility and want to do the best job they can. Teachers are dedicated to helping children learn, nurses to saving lives, and railway workers to keeping passengers safe. Their inner sense of responsibility can create a shared public duty to do the right thing and to try to improve lives in their communities, despite the daily challenges they face.

At times, however, public sector workers, like others, can become demoralised, whether through high workloads, poor working conditions, limited pay rises or bad management. Some of these pressures may be unavoidable, including from the unexpected demands that came with the COVID-19 pandemic. And solving endemic management issues is never easy and can take years of sustained effort. But a demoralised workforce will be less dedicated to their jobs and less likely to provide high-quality public services. It might help focus minds if all public bodies were required to report annually on levels of staff engagement within their organisations. Successful commercial firms, including John Lewis, Standard Chartered Bank, BAE Systems and Toyota, are clear that, if their employees are positively engaged in their business, they then perform better and become more productive. This means establishing respect in the workplace, treating people as individuals and inviting their contributions to solving problems, as advocated by the employers' organisation Engage for Success and others. These lessons could be applied to every public body and the rules of public reporting changed accordingly.

People management can improve too. Performance management is sometimes poor in public bodies. There may be a lack of clarity about who is accountable, with good performance unrecognised and poor performance unpunished. Managers may be too busy or too poorly trained to give good feedback.[1] This can sap organisations and their people, resulting in underperformance and lower productivity. Good performance management motivates people to do their best and to work well with others.[2]

Improving performance management should be at the heart of future public service improvement strategies, and reported in annual reports too. If high performance is expected of everyone and encouraged through good management, then public service leaders can more explicitly be held to account for organisational performance, including by elected politicians in government and on Select Committees.

Effective performance management in public bodies creates a chain of accountability linking everyone paid with public money, from frontline teachers, social workers and civil servants, to their chief executives and boards. They are each responsible for ensuring that public bodies play by the rules, obey the law, spend public money well, and provide public services effectively for communities. These public bodies are then accountable to elected politicians in government and in Parliament who, in turn, through the rules of democracy, are accountable to voters.

This direct chain of accountability creates pressure on public bodies to play by the rules. Like the other rules of democracy, these rules are refereed. In this case, auditors, inspectors and regulators are the referees of public services. They scrutinise spending and services, and publish their findings. The schools regulator Ofsted inspects the quality of teaching and how children are kept active, well fed and safe, while the health regulator the Care Quality Commission inspects hospitals in England, including emergency services and outpatient care. And so on. There are almost 100 such regulators in the UK. Their work makes performance transparent, allowing anyone to compare public services based on independent assessments and robust data.

Public auditors have a similar refereeing role. In the UK, the National Audit Office (NAO), Audit Scotland, Audit Wales and the Northern Ireland Audit Office each check how public bodies have spent public taxes, including that spending is well controlled and that there has been no fraud. Auditors have significant power and can report problems to the police or to Parliament. In November 2018 alone, the NAO published 11 reports, including on income tax, digital electricity and gas meters, employment at the BBC, and spending on schools. The reports were discussed in Parliament and in the media, with decision-makers held to account.

There are also 12 UK ombudsman schemes that receive complaints from anyone who uses public services, balancing the competing views of the complainant and the public body. The Housing Ombudsman helps tenants who have a dispute with their landlord, and the Local Government Ombudsman investigates complaints relating to a range of local public services. And so on.

And there is the backstop of judicial reviews that allow us to seek to challenge the lawfulness of decisions by public bodies including the government. Judges must then decide if the decisions were illegal, unfair or unreasonable. In 2018, for example, of the 3,597 judicial reviews lodged, 184 cases proceeded to a full hearing, and 74 of the decisions challenged were overturned, including 23 decisions made by local authorities and 7 by the police.[3]

These auditors, regulators, ombudsman schemes and the courts are the regulatory authorities that work on our behalf to enforce the rules of democracy as well as the rule of law. Auditors report their findings to politicians on Select Committees, who use the reports to hold public bodies to account for playing by the rules. The committees challenge those responsible for public services to explain failures and describe the actions they will take to make improvements. Most meetings are held in public, and some can be difficult to watch. In 2014, the Public Accounts Committee told the head of the civil service that the Department for Work and Pensions had wasted £566 million of public money on 'the shambles' of a new universal credit welfare system.[4] The committee recommended changes. Those responsible for railways, the health service and defence have been held to account in similar ways.

The scrutiny provided by Select Committees helps to keep public bodies honest and complying with the rules, whether these relate to the public bodies' legal obligations or to their accountability for public money. Only audit offices report directly to them. The committees' important role could be strengthened through closer links with other public service regulators, who are better placed than any to offer politicians impartial, independent views about public service performance, including by identifying problems and good practice.

In addition, it would help Select Committee scrutiny if auditors were given the power to follow public money wherever it is spent, including by commercial companies and charities. By 2010, for example, there were 2,075 secondary schools and 2,440 primary schools that had been moved to the private sector, at a cost to government of £746 million, to become academies. But the NAO's remit does not reach them.[5] As such, the headteacher of a Wakefield school could pay himself £82,000 from public money for three months' work in 2015, and a further £440,000 in consultancy fees to companies he owns, without being held publicly to account.[6] The 716 long-term Private Finance Initiative (PFI) deals struck in health, defence, road building and environment management, costing £10.3 billion in 2017, should also be subject to greater public scrutiny.[7]

Public service ombudsman schemes could also be strengthened. They can take years to resolve complaints and their recommendations can be ignored. Only the Financial Ombudsman Service makes legally binding recommendations. Their work could be better coordinated and promoted, and their findings also reported to Select Committees.[8]

More effective scrutiny could exist locally too. There are no parallels to the national Public Accounts Committee within local democracy, making it harder to scrutinise the performance of schools, clinics and road management. Funding for local services often comes from various sources. This makes it difficult to hold a single organisation or person to account for failure. Weak accountability risks poor public services and wasted public money. Local councils should set up strong, independent Local Public Accounts Committees to replace the function that was performed until 2015 by the Audit Commission.[9]

And in future, a global Public Accounts Committee could scrutinise those who receive public funds internationally, so they, too, play by the rules of democratic accountability and spend public money well on the public's behalf. The committee would publicly examine the spending of the UN, including the ICJ, the World Bank, the WHO, the IAEA and UNESCO. In 2016, they collectively spent US$9 billion on peacekeeping operations, US$3.2 billion on refugees, US$2.5 billion on health, US$4.5 billion on food programmes, and much else. From 2019 to 2021 the UK funded 4.6 per cent of the UN's regular budgets in money raised from domestic taxes. Yet the UN bodies are currently audited from within the UN itself,[10] and their bosses are not publicly held to account for any allegations of waste, excessive bureaucracy or corruption, as they would be if they had to appear before elected politicians with suitable authority, whether at a UN Parliamentary Assembly or a global Public Accounts Committee.

Negative and positive accountability

Strengthening the chain of accountability in public bodies would help to improve how those responsible for public services comply with the rules, and narrow the Accountability Gap between those who pay their taxes and those who spend them.

But public service regulators can do more than hold public bodies to account. As well as identifying those that don't play by the rules, they can also highlight examples of good practice. This will help to improve public services. The rules of democratic accountability focus more on the negative rather than the positive. The inspectors, regulators, auditors and Select Committees that enforce the rules highlight failure more than success, and target areas for development rather than praise achievement. Accountability for public services has come to mean being careful with public money, avoiding mistakes and learning lessons from failure. These are vital. But accountability should encourage good practice as well as prevent bad practice. It should mean praising good value for money, acknowledging projects that are implemented well, and recognising innovation and success under pressure. Through performance management, managers should spot innovation as well as challenge mistakes. In other words, public bodies should be as accountable for improving their services and helping others to improve as they are for spending public money well and avoiding mismanagement.

It is important to hold politicians and other decision-makers to account for their decisions. But in doing so, we not only want them to avoid failure and risk; we also want them to encourage improvement in public services and to ensure that success is quickly replicated. Politicians could also do more to encourage responsible innovation so that public services are provided more effectively and in better ways, with rewards for those who do so.[11]

Looking at problems is understandable. Human brains react more strongly to negative than to positive stimulation as a way to avoid danger and to survive.[12] Our ancestors learned that steering clear of negative things, such as dangerous animals and poisonous plants, was more important than approaching positive things, such as edible roots and shady trees. It is the same today. When walking to the shops, we more quickly spot a car driven erratically than one driven safely by a friend. We are hard-wired to pay more attention to negative than to positive information.

But for public services, a focus on negative accountability is only half the picture. It leads to risk aversion rather than responsible risk-taking. It holds people to account for failure but not for success. The rules of democratic accountability should change so that both are important. Negative accountability is inevitable: ombudsman schemes deal with complaints, not customer satisfaction, and a bad audit or inspection report can stop public services from making the same mistakes again. Positive accountability for success can, in addition, lead to faster and wider improvement.

We learn more through the positive reinforcement of good behaviour than through the criticism of bad behaviour. This is the foundation of longstanding teaching practice in schools and how we help children to learn to walk and talk.[13] Positive reinforcement is the most effective way to train high-performance mountain rescue dogs. It works in experiments with laboratory rats. It works with us. Praise and reward make us feel good, and more likely to repeat positive behaviours again. When positive behaviour becomes embedded and natural, further positive feedback can help us to experiment and try to do things even better.

In contrast, learning is inhibited if we only get negative feedback. If a teacher tells us that we are bad at singing or at maths, it is harder to keep going despite the criticism. When we get negative feedback, we can become mentally and physically defensive. This closes our mind to different options. We hesitate and maybe give up. When we think about something we can do well, we probably remember a parent or a teacher who praised and encouraged us. They told us that we were good, and that they liked our songs or our sums. They encouraged us to keep going and to get better. Public services would benefit from the power of positive feedback in the same way, including in the way they are held to account.

Learning organisations

Positive feedback benefits organisations as well as individuals. The best commercial firms constantly learn. If they do not, they fail. Over US$476 billion was spent on research and development in the US in 2018, representing 2.7 per cent of GDP. The proportions are similar elsewhere, with €320 billion spent on research across the EU in 2018. Amazon spent US$22.6 billion on research in 2018, with another 12 companies spending over US$10 billion each.[14] These companies understand that they must invest in learning from what has gone well, and what has not, so that they can adapt to change, or they will fall behind their competitors and go out of business.

Some companies make it their mission to learn and improve. The science and technology firm 3M spends around 6 per cent of its revenue on research, and generates a third of its sales from products introduced in the last five years.[15] Other firms make a virtue of copying others. As soon as a new product comes to market, whether a toy, sports shoe or mobile phone, some firms immediately take it apart, copy it and start competing. The Chinese fashion chain Miniso launched in 2013 by copying Japanese competitors Uniqlo and Muji. Within three years it had 1,500 stores across Southeast Asia.

Firms that fail to innovate may even collapse. Kodak once dominated the market for camera film. In the early 1980s, it sold 90 per cent of all film bought in the US. But the company was slow to meet the challenge of digital photography, preferring to sell existing products than to develop new ones. In 2012 it went bankrupt. Nokia fared similarly. In 1999 there were more Nokia phones sold than any others in the world and the company was making US$4 billion profit a year. But it failed to respond to the launch of Apple's iPhone, thinking customers would not leave a trusted brand. By 2013 the company was sold to Microsoft for a tenth of its earlier value.[16]

Managers across the world are familiar with these and other stories of corporate success and failure. They know that the future of their firm already exists, but somewhere else. They just have to find and copy it. They must compete hard to succeed. This involves learning. Leading companies in each sector are 40 per cent more productive than the average firm.[17] The best companies adapt to changes in their operating environment and meet the changing needs of their customers. They invest time and money in research and in experimentation. And they award bonuses and promotions to employees who develop new capabilities and take appropriate risks.

Because of this existential need for companies to learn in order to survive, a massive international infrastructure helps commercial firms and their employees to learn effectively, including from good practice wherever it exists. There are hundreds of business schools around the world. INSEAD, based in Paris and Singapore, the top-ranked business school by the *Financial Times* in 2021,[18] has 1,400 students on Master of Business Administration courses paying €81,000 each, as well as over 11,000 executives on short learning programmes.

In addition, a thousand business books are published worldwide every month. Dale Carnegie's book *How to win friends and influence people* has sold 15 million copies, and Stephen Covey's book *The 7 habits of highly effective people* has sold 25 million copies. In the nine months to December 2017, 7.1 million business books were sold in the US, earning their authors and publishers US$169 million, with a further US$58 million from the sale of 5.2 million business books in an audio or electronic format. Sales are supplemented by talks. Simon Sinek's TED talk on leadership has been viewed over 26 million times. Hundreds of companies offer online training in business skills. The US business education market in 2017 was worth an estimated US$135 billion.[19]

And there is an industry of analysts looking at company performance for investors. There are over 900,000 financial, business and stock market analysts in the US alone. They review data from sales, profits, customers and demography to determine which companies are doing well and which could do better. Strong commercial performance is rewarded immediately: investors buy their stocks and consumers their products.

Commercial firms know that they must keep learning, both from their own experience and from their competitors. Most of all, they must learn from their customers. If they learn well, they will adapt to new environments and new challenges by improving their products and services. If their services don't improve, they won't survive.

Learning for public services

This extensive learning infrastructure to benefit commercial firms is virtually nonexistent for public services. Some universities teach public administration, but they train fewer students than business schools. The French École nationale d'administration, INSEAD's public sector equivalent, takes only 110 students a year. Fewer students and lower fees mean less research about what works to improve public services. And there are few management gurus or books to improve the skills needed specifically to work in public services,[20] including dealing with the politics, the media and the users of services who are often in dire straits and who usually cannot be charged a fee. This makes it hard for public service managers to find out how to improve by studying examples from elsewhere.

Many public bodies train their staff well. But training budgets are under pressure, including in the NHS, where funding shortfalls had led to gaps in trained staff even before COVID-19 arrived.[21] The National School of Government at Sunningdale was closed in 2011 after running at a loss. Professional bodies help to plug this learning gap. The Chartered Institute of Library and Information Professionals, the Chartered Institute of Public Finance and Accountancy and the Royal College of Paediatrics and Child Health, among hundreds of other professional associations, run courses, conferences and seminars to help people to progress their careers and learn from each other. They also produce professional journals. But these programmes are piecemeal and can be of mixed quality. They rely on public service workers motivating themselves to continue their professional development and to invest their time and often their own money too.

For commercial firms, learning is about life or death. For public services, it is something nice to have if they can afford it. Or it is remedial: staff are given training to fix something wrong, not to think new things and grow. In the marketplace, the power of competition leads to constant innovation, efficiency and learning as firms struggle to survive and grow. But public services often have no competitors. And they survive even if they perform badly or fail. Poorly run railways stay open, and sick people will still be treated even by poorly trained medical staff lacking supplies.

Yet public services are full of knowledge about what works to improve what they do. What's the best way to reduce re-offending? Or to speed recovery after surgery? Or to support children with dyslexia? Or to process parking fines? There is good practice in all these areas, somewhere. But it is hard to locate. In fact, those working in public services may have little idea where to find out what the best in their sector looks like, so they can copy it. There may be something in a professional journal or at a conference, for those with the time and money to look. But audit and inspection reports tend to show only what has gone wrong, without wider learning being drawn together. And the tools of data analysis are at best embryonic in public services, despite the vast quantities of information they collectively hold about social needs.

The lack of a basic learning infrastructure for public services is a big missed opportunity for improvement. And its absence makes even less sense because all those working in public services are on the same side, working to improve their communities.

The lack of competition between public services means, in theory, that there should be no impediment to public bodies sharing learning with each other about what works best. Significant improvements in public services could be achieved in principle simply by replicating existing best practice everywhere else, if only people could easily identify what best practice in their field is. They could then implement it themselves, giving every public service a better chance of performing at the level of the best. Public services that learn will improve faster and spend less public money.

Improvement through copying will not happen on its own. Public services do not have the same hunger for profit, or fear of ruin, that drives businesses to learn from others and apply lessons to improve their own performance. Commercial markets distribute good-quality, timely information and learning about success, as if by Adam Smith's invisible hand. Public services, in contrast, often think that they can get by fine by doing what they've always done.

Instead, the rules of accountability for public bodies should be strengthened so that all organisations in receipt of public funds are obliged to share learning about what works best to improve public services so others can copy it. As this learning cannot be shared by the invisible hand of the marketplace, it may need to be a requirement of receiving public money. One case study from each public body each year could quickly create a large pool of data and good practice. Regulators, inspectorates and auditors are well placed to report the positive as well as the negative findings of their work. With the global computing power now available, fully anonymised data on public service performance could be made freely available in formats that can be analysed by researchers in universities and think tanks.

A shared public service learning infrastructure along these lines could hold and analyse knowledge for all public bodies to benefit from, providing up-to-date information about how to use limited funding as effectively as possible to run public services well. Although potentially expensive, this learning infrastructure would cost less to establish than the billions spent on commercial research and development. Businesses believe the investment to be worthwhile; it may prove to be no different for public services. And it may save the hidden costs paid today in public services failing to implement good practice and innovations, and underperforming and repeating others' mistakes as a consequence. The failed rehabilitation of prisoners, the missed learning opportunities for children and preventable deaths all cost money too.

Changing the rules of democratic accountability so learning is shared, as a requirement of receiving public money, would help public services to learn and improve. Good negative accountability means holding public services to account for poor performance, for losing money and for causing harm. Good positive accountability would mean holding them to account for learning from performance elsewhere, and for sharing learning with others. Public services, unlike commercial firms, are not in competition with each other. Indeed, they must collaborate and work in trusted partnerships to achieve their goals. Learning should come naturally to public service staff, if it is encouraged and nurtured.

Combining negative with positive accountability would recognise success. It might also lead to praise for politicians such as Barbara Castle who introduced equal pay legislation in 1970, Michael Heseltine who, from 1981, developed London's docklands into a financial district, and David Blunkett who, from 1997, improved school literacy rates. Successful politicians deserve recognition too.

Building a learning infrastructure along these lines would make it easier for public services to improve and achieve more than they could without the lessons of others' experience. And it would help to close the Expectation Gap between what we want from public services in our community, and what they actually provide.

A new phase for public services

Public services, like democracy, have evolved before. Until the Industrial Revolution, public services in communities were not provided beyond the maintenance of order through custom or force. Religious institutions and charities looked after some of the needy. But people mostly had to look after their own, including those too young, too old or too sick to look after themselves.

With the Industrial Revolution, expectations of public services started to rise. People wanted safer streets, cleaner air, education for their children and care for their elderly. Ad hoc support from the family was no longer enough. This phase of public services, which, in the UK, lasted to around 1980, created the basic infrastructure that communities needed. Roads, railways and sewerage systems were built. And police forces, schools and hospices were established to protect and provide for all members of a local community, and not only those who could afford them. Public services were nationalised and standardised, and eventually became universal. But they remained modest. Health services were available to all, but focused on providing advice, antibiotics and emergency treatment. Education was available to all, too, but in the UK in 1980 only 7 per cent of each age cohort went to university. Many services were rationed or not available. Our grandparents expected to have access to public services, but their expectations were not high. Having just escaped poverty or war, they were grateful for any public healthcare or education that they could get.

But those born from the 1950s onwards became less satisfied with what their parents and grandparents had received. They came to want more from life in increasingly prosperous communities. Public services strained to keep pace with these postwar social changes and to rising expectations and increased demands.

Thus, from 1980, a new phase of public services began in the UK that drew on commercial experience and the power of the market. Public utilities, including electricity, gas and water, were privatised, as were the state-owned firms making cars, trains and aeroplanes. Management techniques were also imported into public bodies. There were investments in technology. Inspectorates started to regulate public services, producing league tables to compare public bodies against indicators and targets to improve performance. Some public services were provided by commercial and voluntary bodies. And public services were encouraged to think of their users as customers.

These approaches and techniques, generally known as 'new public management',[22] helped to improve public services. Data, evidence, national standards and professional development have ensured that the quality of public services is more consistent across communities. Inspectorates and regulators identify and tackle poor performance. And people mostly do not care if their public services are run by private, public or voluntary sector organisations, as long as they are available when needed and of good-enough quality. In these ways, public services have partially responded to the greater diversity of modern communities and to increased expectations.

But these improvements are no longer enough to address today's challenges, particularly now that the Global Technological Revolution has given us a greater choice of fast commercial services always available online. Levels of public service funding are unlikely to match the money available to big online firms, and many public services have less money now than they did before the economic crisis of 2008.[23] As a consequence, public services can struggle to meet local needs.

Today's dilemma is how to keep improving public services without pumping in vast quantities of new money. Incremental, marginal improvements, such as those delivered by the techniques of new public management, are important. But they may be insufficient or too slow to meet fast-growing expectations. The next phase of public service improvement may therefore need to better exploit data and information management to maximise the potential of the millions of dedicated staff working in public services. The tools created by the Global Technological Revolution, including online platforms to share data, information and knowledge, can help to improve public services if encouraged to do so by a new rule of democracy, such that: 'All organisations receiving taxes must be accountable both for how they spend public money and for sharing their learning and good practice'.

This and other new rules of democracy may together narrow the Accountability Gap between those making decisions about tax-funded services and those who benefit from them, including through:

- A holistic system of democracy where accountability for public services sits where the services are experienced, whether at local, national or international level.
- Full visibility of how taxes are raised and spent on public services, so taxpayers can influence how their money is distributed.
- A guaranteed basic level of provision that should be expected from public services.
- Stronger chains of democratic accountability within public services.
- Public bodies and regulators sharing learning about public service improvement.
- Rules to ensure that politicians and other decision-makers, locally, nationally and internationally, are more accountable for their decisions.

New rules of democracy could encourage guaranteed minimum standards of public services that elected politicians would be accountable for providing. From this base, public services would access learning from the best in their sectors, enabling good practice to be copied and innovation nurtured. This would help to increase the accountability of public services, politicians and other decision-makers, giving communities greater influence over decisions that impact on them. And public services that are visibly trying to improve may also help to narrow the Expectation Gap between what we want from public services and what we get.

But all gaps have two sides to them. On the one side, politicians and other decision-makers should be more accountable for improving the performance of public services. But on the other side of the gap is us. Our expectations of public services, and of decision-makers, are higher than before. It may be unreasonable for us simply to wait for others to change without taking any action ourselves.

We can also narrow the gap by managing down our own expectations. We are right to expect public services to improve, and politicians to be accountable for them. But we may need to expect less from public services than we get from online services. This might mean accepting lower guaranteed standards of public services than the immediate service we get online. With more knowledge of how our taxes are raised and spent, such as through a personal online tax account, we may also come to have more realistic expectations about the kind of public services we can get for our money, unless we want to pay more in tax. We must take some accountability ourselves.

7

The rules for us

Effective democracy means politicians and public services playing by the rules, including new rules to respond to the challenges of the Global Technological Revolution. We must play by the rules of democracy too.

Whoever we are, we share our community. We live on the same streets as our neighbours, use the same electricity supply as others in our region, and share our environment with everyone on the planet. This means that we also depend on each other, as we will be personally impacted by other people's behaviour if they break the rules. As a further response to the challenges of the Global Technological Revolution, it may be necessary to make explicit our own obligation to play by the rules too, such as in a rule of democracy that states:

> Each member of a community must adhere to the rule of law and the rules of democracy, including by paying taxes, voting and contributing time and money to their community.

Although we may be happier applying new rules to politicians than to ourselves, we are already subject to the rule of law, as well as to less explicit rules, including accepted social norms of behaviour. Rules help communities get by and prosper, and reduce the conflict of disagreement. We live by rules from birth. As children, we accept that others set rules that we must obey. Parents tell us to clean our teeth; teachers tell us to be quiet in class. Laws state that we cannot drive before we are 17 or buy alcohol before we are 18. As adults, we may agree with the rules of our community, or we may not, but we know that if we do not adhere to the rules, there will be certain consequences.

Rules, whether laws or norms of behaviour, help communities to run themselves effectively. In a village or housing estate, implicit rules may require residents to keep their doorstep or front garden clean, or let children play only in certain places. Some communities require prospective residents to agree formally to such rules before they can live there. Implicit rules and norms of behaviour exist in cities too, although they may be harder to see.[1] Explicit rules, on the other hand, including the law of the land, are often very visible and are generally enforced by authorised, uniformed officials, including the police.

Living in a community, whether a village or our shared global community, means living by agreed rules – laws and social norms – and knowing that we may be sanctioned if we do not. Playing by agreed rules is also important because we all stand to benefit from ordered, safe communities, and from public services that would be impossible to organise individually.

Obeying the law and paying taxes

In all communities, rules change over time, with new rules created and others abolished. In democracies, we give our authority to politicians to represent our interests and to agree changes to the rules on our behalf. This is how the game of democracy is played. Through the application of agreed rules of debate and decision-making, democracies can make fundamental changes to the way they are organised and the rules that everyone must adhere to. In 2018, for example, 66 per cent of voters in a referendum in Ireland decided to legalise abortion, while in Argentina in the same year, elected politicians voted 38 to 31 against the same change, voting to reverse this decision in 2021. In 28 countries, including Brazil, Finland, South Africa and Taiwan, there have been votes to allow same-sex marriages, while in 34 other countries, including Jamaica, Poland and Cambodia, there are laws to prevent people from getting married to someone of the same sex. In all these cases, the rules are agreed by the politicians of the communities concerned, and on their behalf.

Whatever rules a community has agreed, and until they are changed, we are obliged to adhere to them. They apply equally to everyone. We will be punished if we do not obey the law, maybe by a fine or imprisonment. Yet, in democracies, we are free to campaign, on our own, in groups and through politicians, to change the rules and the punishments associated with breaking them.

All communities have rules. Respecting the rule of law is well established. We want others to obey the law so that we do not suffer from their selfishness, antisocial behaviour or recklessness. Obeying the law is how the rules of democracy apply to us.

We have a similar obligation to pay our taxes. Politicians set rules on our behalf, including how public services should be paid for. We are entitled to benefit from public services, including clean air, sanitation, education and defence. We must pay for them. We may disagree with the way we are taxed, just as we may disagree with other rules in our community, and we can campaign to change them. But until taxes are changed, we should not avoid paying them. We expect others to pay their taxes. We should too. This rule of democracy applies to us as well.

Changing communities

More could be done to strengthen the rules of democracy that apply to us. The Global Technological Revolution has accelerated changes to the nature of community ties, weakening the sense of obligation and mutual accountability to one other, while raising expectations of public services.

We live in overlapping communities. We have a local physical community, including the street where we live, and our national identity and its community too. We also live in online communities, including professional communities and communities of interest. And the Global Technological Revolution has made it more evident than ever that we share trade rules, the internet, the environment and much else in a single global community with everyone else on the planet.

Some of these are recent changes. But communities began changing fundamentally 200 years ago with the Industrial

Revolution. Adults and their families left the intimate community life of their village to migrate to cities seeking work. The same trend, of industrialisation followed by urbanisation, has been repeated across Africa, Asia and the Americas. Around 4.2 billion people now live in urban areas, about 55 per cent of the world's population. And while city dwellers may feel a shared sense of community within their immediate neighbourhood, they have less sense of shared community with those on the other side of town. Looser social ties in modern communities make it harder to share accountability with others for problems within a community and to be held to account for playing by the rules. We may feel a shared responsibility to keep our immediate neighbourhood clean, but who cares if we drop a plastic bottle far from home where no one knows us?[2]

The Global Technological Revolution has weakened the sense of shared accountability to those in the same physical space. Geographical communities matter less. We work and socialise online with people we will never meet. On a bus or train, we may feel more connected to our digital friend a thousand miles away than to the flesh-and-blood person sitting next to us. When choosing where to live, access to a fast internet connection is now near the top of the list of our requirements.

But in other ways, the Global Technological Revolution has strengthened the sense of community. We may belong to an online group with others who share our religion, our sexuality, our passion for John Donne's poems or for saving the planet. These are not physical communities, but communities nonetheless. In them, we share not only interests and information, but also responsibilities, giving and receiving mutual support, and making decisions about our group and its future. Digital and geographical communities can overlap: we may be members of an online group to preserve local heritage or to keep a local park clean. And we connect with others across the planet on issues of our choice, creating new communities that cross local and national geographical boundaries.

Each of these communities is a system. We are members of many systems, and we have an interest in these systems being run effectively. The systems are complex, with the thousands or millions of people in them interacting with each other in an almost infinite number of ways. Yet our own interaction with these systems is often transactional and intended only to achieve short-term goals.[3] The individualistic, digital world created by the Global Technological Revolution has encouraged us to expect to meet our needs whenever we want. We press our screens to make a purchase, connect with friends or see a film. We may want to get on with our lives without bothering or being bothered by the people around us. We may not know our neighbours, or be interested in them.

Yet we are still flesh-and-blood people who depend on public services to live our daily lives — we, and others in our geographical community, are collectively responsible for them, and, like it or not, we pay for them through our taxes.

And public services are fundamentally unlike commercial services. They are rarely digital and anonymous, like Amazon, Apple or Uber Eats. Nor are they delivered by providers who compete for our money. In most cases, we cannot choose which police force keeps us safe, which air we breathe or which road we drive on. And public services are communal services too. If you buy this pizza or that car from a commercial provider, no one much cares about your choice. But people's choices in a community impact on each other more directly, as part of a complex system. If my neighbour throws their rubbish on my street, or smokes on the train I am on, or sends their child to my kids' school, then their choices affect me. Their choices may create costs that my taxes must pay for, such as the cost of clearing up their rubbish or of recruiting more local teachers. And my choices impact similarly on them.

As such we cannot simply be passive recipients of public services, as we are with the commercial services that we buy with our own money. We cannot help but be connected to others in our geographical community, and share responsibility with them, even if we don't know them. Better communities are not delivered like pizza. They are built collectively by people living in specific places, and who care about improving where they live. Public services are provided in a geographical community, often by members of the same community, and they are paid for by the community too. They belong to our community and they are personal. Together we need to feel more accountable individually and collectively for their success or failure.

Participating in communities by voting

Obeying the law and paying taxes are largely passive acts. Playing by these rules of democracy does not require much engagement with others. But because public services are communal services, with each personal choice impacting on others, members of a community cannot, and perhaps should not, detach themselves completely from their community and delegate its management only to others. We may have no interest in commercial services that other people buy, whether a motorboat or a microwave, but we cannot help but have an interest in public services. They inevitably impact on each of us, whether now or in future. And we pay for them. We have a strong vested interest in their success.

In representative democracies, rather than require everyone to spend their time agreeing in detail how public services should be funded and managed, we periodically elect politicians to make decisions on our behalf. Because the decisions can be complex or technical, we trust them and the institutions they manage, knowing that we can hold them to account if necessary.

But in many democracies, some people decide not to choose a representative. In the US throughout the 20th century, around 60 per cent of eligible adults vote in presidential elections. In Europe, 75 per cent of the electorate voted in the 2017 French presidential election, and 69 per cent in the 2017 UK General Election. These are high figures. Only 40 per cent of US citizens tend to vote in state or local elections, with 37 per cent voting in the 2014 mid-term elections. Since 1945, an average of only 54 per cent of eligible citizens voted in national elections across Central and South America. There are also differences between groups within a community. In the 2017 UK General Election, there were few differences in turnout by ethnicity, but large differences by age, with 80 per cent of those aged over 60 voting but only 43 per cent of those aged between 18 and 24.[4]

Other countries choose a different path. In Australia, voting has been compulsory since 1924, resulting in a turnout of over

91 per cent. Voting is also compulsory in 21 other countries including Belgium, Brazil and Bolivia. In some of these countries, there are sanctions or fines for not voting. In Australia the fee is AU$20, and the potential loss of a driving licence or ineligibility for some public service jobs for repeated failure to vote without good cause.[5] A further way to narrow the growing Accountability Gap may be to consider evolving the UK's rules of democracy to require compulsory voting too.

There are strong arguments against compulsory voting. Free societies allow us to be free not to vote, and we should not be coerced into doing so. Voting has been considered a right by some, rather than an obligation. And requiring us to vote at risk of a sanction might be considered an infringement of our liberty and undemocratic in itself.[6] But if democracy is to overcome the challenges it currently faces, voting in future may need to be thought of as an obligation and not as a right, akin to paying taxes or obeying the law. We are members of a community, including a shared global community. We can choose to be a member of different communities, but we cannot be a member of none. This gives us obligations.

Choosing not to vote has an impact on others. Sometimes there are difficult decisions to make. Our community may need more electricity. To get it, we must either bulldoze some people's homes to make way for a hydroelectric dam, or clear other people's fields to install solar panels, or do without the extra power. Someone must make the decision on everyone's behalf. The person who does so should represent everyone's views, even though the decision is hard, and some will oppose it. It is understandable if we sometimes want to hide from hard decisions like these, by sitting on the fence or not participating. Then there are others to blame if things go wrong.

Imagine eight friends are hungry. Three are vegan, but two want beef burgers. The remaining three friends don't mind and are reluctant to upset either the meat-eaters or the vegans by taking sides. The group votes three-to-two to go to a vegan restaurant. Those not voting allow others with the strongest views to decide something that affects everyone. The meat-eaters, and perhaps the vegans too, may feel let down by those who were not prepared to share the responsibility for perhaps finding a place where beef burgers and vegan food are both on the menu.

Similarly, in democracies such as the UK, the future of many communities is decided by those who vote more, who tend to be older and more politically committed. And without international democracy, those in rich countries have more influence over global decision-making than those who don't. Those in undemocratic countries have even less influence or none at all.

Politicians are required to make difficult decisions about complex issues and to manage public services on our behalf. They cannot meet our community's needs, or even know what the needs are, if they are not told what we prefer. The rules of democracy may therefore need to require us to vote in elections to tell them.

Voting may be inconvenient. But most democracies allow votes to be cast in advance or by post, as has been the case in Australia since 1877 and in the UK since 1920. Some US municipalities, including in Oregon and Washington, use postal votes exclusively, and voters can drop off their ballots at election stations in person if they wish; exceptions are made for those who are ill and have a medical certificate. Some countries apply an age limit. In Luxembourg voting is optional over the age of 75, and in Argentina and Brazil over the age of 70. Online voting systems are becoming more secure, private, accurate and auditable, and have been used in Brazil, Estonia, India and Malaysia, although they remain riskier than in-person voting.[7]

Voting is for everyone, whatever their circumstances or background. India is a democracy with 864 million voters. Over 66 per cent of the electorate turn out to vote, including around 128 million Indians who struggle to read and write. Turnout is higher in rural, less educated areas than in cities. The same is the case in African elections.[8]

Every vote makes a difference, even if an ideal candidate is not available. Those who do not vote allow others in their community with more extreme or entrenched views to make decisions on behalf of everyone. A community where everyone votes may encourage politicians to pander less to those with marginal but strongly held views, but who vote, and more to the undecided members of their community who may otherwise not vote at all. This may make it harder for extremists to be elected and for politics to become polarised.

A vote also matters because politicians are highly attuned to changes of opinion. In 1972 the first Green Party was formed in Tasmania, Australia, to fight deforestation and local environmental damage. It won 3 per cent of the vote. Green parties formed elsewhere and, by 2016, a Green candidate won the Austrian presidential election and in August 2021 formed part of a coalition government in Scotland. As importantly, candidates from other political parties noted the change of mood. Many adopted Green policies such that few candidates now ignore environmental issues.[9] In another example, in 2015, 3.9 million people voted for the United Kingdom Independence Party (UKIP). They only elected one MP, Douglas Carswell, in Essex, but their voice was heard. The Conservative Party promised a referendum on whether to take the UK out of the EU, and UKIP decided not to compete against most Conservative candidates in the December 2019 General Election.

Compulsory voting may make it easier to apply the rules of democracy more fairly and make democracy itself more effective. Electoral fraud could be harder if voters are not put off by being without the right paperwork. And politicians may spend less time persuading potential voters to register and turn out at polling stations, and more time focusing on issues and persuading members of their community to vote for them rather than for someone else. A change to the rules of democracy along these lines may make democracy more effective by helping politicians to be more representative of their communities and more responsive to their needs.

Committing to our communities

Voting helps make it clear that we, too, are responsible for the success of our community. The growing Accountability Gap might also narrow further if we contribute directly to our own communities.

According to the UN, an estimated 970 million people around the world regularly volunteer their help to others.[10]

They work at times of emergency, such as to respond to fires or floods, but also each week in schools and clinics to support their communities. They add value worth US$1.3 trillion a year. In the US, 25 per cent of all adults volunteer on average 32 hours a year, worth an estimated US$184 billion. France has 200,000 volunteer fire officers, and Finland a reported 610,000 volunteers who support children's sports teams. In the UK, around 36 per cent of adults volunteered with a group or organisation at least once in 2018. Of these 19.4 million people, around 12 million volunteered at least once a month.[11] These include the 370,000 volunteer school governors who provide support and oversight for headteachers, the 12,000 regular volunteers who help the Royal Society for the Protection of Birds to spot and manage endangered species, and the 57,000 volunteers working with the National Trust to promote and preserve UK heritage. The value of this to the UK has been calculated to be worth well over £100 billion a year.[12]

Since 1985, the UN and others have promoted an International Volunteer Day[13] to encourage people to contribute to improving their communities. If the rules of democracy in future were to strongly encourage each of us to contribute, say, 45 minutes of our time each week (or five days a year) to improving our community, this might generate extra value worth over £200 billion, and be the equivalent of millions of additional staff improving our communities.

Many already donate money to charities too. In the US, between 3 and 5 per cent of the average family income goes to charity, with those on low incomes tending to give more, as a proportion of their salaries, than the rich. On one measure the US is the most generous country in the world, while in nine other countries, including the UK, over 65 per cent of people give money at least once a year. In the UK, charities receive around £10 billion a year in donations, with 64 per cent of UK residents giving at least once a year and 24 per cent every month. The average monthly donation is £45.[14]

Giving to charities is immensely personal: 19 per cent of all UK donations in 2018 went to religious foundations and 10 per cent to research specific medical conditions. Encouraging more people to give to public services as well as to charities, even just 1 per cent of income per month, could bring an extra £5 billion or more a year to improving UK communities. The money might support schools, hospitals, flood defences or even local police officers, as we prefer. Public services would be accountable for spending donations in the same way that they are already accountable to Parliament for spending other public money.

Changing the rules of democracy to encourage all adults to give time and money to their communities might be considered an illiberal intrusion on personal liberty. Yet many already volunteer and donate. Encouraging this as an expected norm of good social behaviour could bring benefits.

Public services would have more resources, potentially amounting to millions of hours of labour every month and billions of extra pounds a year. The investment of an individual's time and money might also build greater commitment to communities and a greater shared interest in their success and improvement. People may even make friends with others who share their commitments, helping to reduce loneliness and build a greater shared sense of investment in shared communities. Study after study reports the happiness and joy that many get from volunteering, receiving a 'helper's high' when they do good or provide assistance to someone else.[15]

By investing time and money in their communities, its members may also build a deeper understanding of the demands on public services, and how difficult it can be to meet them. In other words, direct involvement in public services may lower expectations. By spending time in local schools, clinics, parks, libraries or train stations, members of a community might see more clearly from first-hand experience how hard most people in public services work, what they have to contend with, and often how little money they have to spend. We may come to realise that not everything we want from public services is possible.

The financial, operational, philosophical and political obstacles to changing social norms so that we all feel obliged to contribute our time and money to our communities are many and large. Compelling community service onto young people has been found to weaken rather than strengthen their community ties, with the exact design of volunteering programmes critical to their success.[16] But the idea has supporters too, including former Bank of England governor Mark Carney in 2021.[17] And, like other proposals in this book, it is just one possible solution to some of the social challenges brought about by the Global Technological Revolution.

A community covenant

Together, these requirements – that we obey the law, vote, pay taxes and contribute to our community – could be formalised into a new rule of democracy. This might recognise and make explicit the obligations that we have to others in our shared communities.

In 1762, Jean-Jacques Rousseau described a social contract[18] between the state and individuals where we each surrender certain individual freedoms in exchange for wider protection and social order. We gain rights for ourselves by accepting our obligations to respect the rights of others, giving up some freedoms to do so. This social contract may now need to be updated to reflect the changes brought by the Global Technological Revolution. A new rule of democracy may need to revise this social contract or create a new community covenant to make clearer the accountability that every member of a community has to others to ensure that the community as a whole, whether locally, nationally or internationally, is governed well, not only by holding politicians to account for their decisions, but by contributing meaningfully to our communities too.

Changing social norms and patterns of behaviour, such as by changing the rules of democracy to create a new community covenant along these lines, may take generations. But there are many examples of significant social and behavioural change that happened in part through changes to the rules. In the 1950s, few people believed that wearing seatbelts in cars would save lives. Most drivers and passengers did not. The first law to make the installation of seatbelts compulsory was in Wisconsin in the US in 1961. Drivers and passengers resisted using them, but attitudes began to change as evidence of their impact mounted, including a 45 per cent reduction in road deaths when seatbelts were worn. Then, starting in 1971 in Japan and in 1972 in Australia, it became compulsory to wear seatbelts. There was resistance, and laws were not enforced. In the 1980s, fines began to be imposed on those caught driving without seatbelts. Today, the wearing of seatbelts in cars has become socially accepted, not just for drivers, but for passengers too. Indeed, we are challenged by family or friends if we do not 'buckle up'. The behaviour is enforced by peer pressure, but facilitated by changes in the law, and the evidence that people have been spared death and injury.

Changing the rules we live by, whether the law of the land, implicit social norms or the rules of democracy, is never straightforward. We often want others, particularly politicians, to resolve difficult problems for us without having to do anything ourselves. But when problems relate to our own community, we may need to do more personally to contribute to solutions, including by voting, and contributing to improving communities with our time and money. And if everyone else plays by these rules, then we are more likely to play by the rules too, just as we now routinely use seatbelts in cars when once we did not.

Putting such rules in place would make our communities more fully accountable: elected politicians who are accountable for decisions that impact on the whole community; public services that are held to account by a Parliament supported by regulators; and members of communities who actively play by the rules of democracy and accountability too.

We share our communities, and we share accountability for making sure that they are successful and thrive, whether the community is our neighbourhood, our nation or our planet.

Narrowing the Expectation Gap

The suggestions in this book attempt to find ways to narrow the Expectation Gap that has grown as a result of the Global Technological Revolution, where we want more from public services than they are sometimes able to deliver. The Expectation Gap can be narrowed on the one side by improving the benefits provided by tax-funded public services:

- International democracy would allow us to elect accountable politicians to act on our behalf to increase the benefits and reduce the harms of international trade, environmental protection and the internet.
- Greater responsibility for politicians managing public services locally would allow us more easily to hold local decision-makers to account for their improvement.
- Strengthening the accountability of all politicians would encourage them to improve public services more in line with our expectations.
- Greater scrutiny of politicians and decision-makers, particularly by Select Committees, would put more effective pressure on those running public services to improve them.
- A personal online tax account would give us information to pressure politicians to spend public money well to achieve improvements.
- A public service learning infrastructure would help good practice to spread quickly from high-performing public services to others.
- Encouraging donations of money and time from everyone would increase the resources available to public services in communities.

The Expectation Gap could also be narrowed on the other side by reducing our expectations of public services:

- More transparent taxation would enable us to see more clearly where our taxes are spent, and how many public services must be funded with how much money, so that, if we really want public services to improve, we may need to pay more in taxes, or expect less.
- Changing the rules of democracy for politicians may help them to meet their promises more, and fib less, discouraging them from raising our expectations beyond what is reasonable.
- Basic standards of public services might be guaranteed, but at a level below our ideal aspirations.
- Encouragement to become more involved in public services may help us to see in our own community how hard it is to provide high-quality services with the money available.

- And a more explicit understanding that public services are not the same as commercial services might teach us that, if we do not contribute to improving public services ourselves, we cannot unreasonably expect them to improve.

These measures to narrow the Expectation Gap are represented in Figure 7.1.

Public services have improved since the 1980s, but not as fast as our expectations. They will no doubt continue to improve, even though money is tight and demand high, and even with the long-term financial and social consequences of the COVID-19 pandemic. For that, we can generally thank the dedication of public service workers, the ongoing positive impact of technological change, and the leadership of politicians and senior public service leaders attempting to resolve complex social problems on our behalf. We can do more ourselves, too, including by fulfilling our accountabilities to others in our community and perhaps also by managing down our expectations of what is reasonable and realistic for public services to provide to our communities with the tax funding available.

Figure 7.1: Narrowing the Expectation Gap of public services

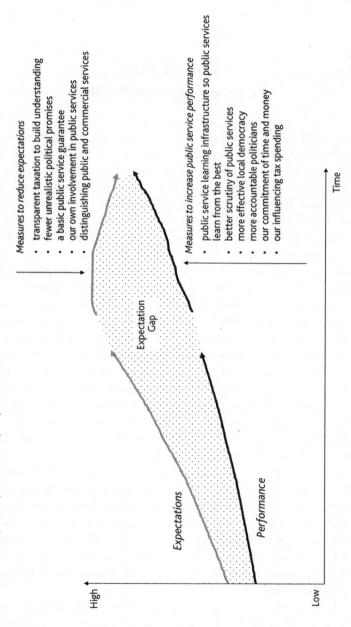

Conclusion:
Refereeing democracy

In this book I have argued that, by profoundly transforming our communities in so many ways, the Global Technological Revolution has contributed to widespread social concerns, including about the perceived threat of global trade and immigration to community identity, the fear of environmental disaster and cyber-crime, and anxieties about the power of tech giants and about the nature of international capitalism itself.

These concerns manifest in different and complex ways. But they are all made worse by a gap in accountability between those who make decisions that impact on our lives and us. Many people, from Australian Prime Minister Scott Morrison to Swedish environmental activist Greta Thunberg, are frustrated that we have little influence over those who run global businesses and technology firms, or over those who damage the environment.[1]

This Accountability Gap has been compounded by an Expectation Gap. The internet has given us instant access to everything. We want for our family and our own community the education, health, safety and social support that we see elsewhere, on our screens. Some people, including in anti-capitalist movements, as espoused by Indian author and activist Arundhati Roy, argue that it is unfair that a global elite is benefiting disproportionately from globalisation and technology, that commercial companies exploit personal data, destroy forests and seas, and pay no tax, and that nothing is done to protect the interests of ordinary people.[2] They, and others, including British Prime Minister Boris Johnson, albeit for very different reasons, say that they want to take back control of decisions made elsewhere.[3]

Demonstrations, marches, petitions, charities, social movements and other group and individual actions, both online and in real life, all play their parts in helping people's voices to be heard by decision-makers. In undemocratic countries, these voices can be ignored, as they were in Belarus and Hong Kong in 2020 and in Russia and Myanmar in 2021.[4] People's voices are more likely to be heard in democracies, where elected politicians depend on addressing the concerns of voters to stay in power.

In these countries, the way to have influence over decisions that impact on people's lives, and to 'take back control', is through democracy itself. It is humanity's most complex social innovation. Democracy gives people control. It allows us to choose who makes decisions on our behalf, and it allows us to change our mind too. Democracy makes decision-makers accountable.

Narrowing the Accountability Gap

But democracy must now evolve to narrow the Accountability Gap that is generating dissatisfaction, resentment and anger. This may mean changing the rules of democracy, just as the rules of democracy were changed following the major social upheaval of the Industrial Revolution 200 years ago.

In practice, this would involve directly electing international politicians, so that all communities of the world are fairly represented in a global parliament that has the authority to hold multinational firms to account, ensure they pay their taxes and look after the environment. It would also involve having local politicians with more power and accountability for the public services in each community, as well as national politicians who, in addition to their other responsibilities, could champion our identities and protect us from discrimination.

Changing the rules of democracy should also entail greater tax transparency so we can have more influence over how public money is taken and then spent to benefit our communities. And it could mean tightening the rules of democracy for politicians, to discourage lying and cheating and to encourage them to meet their promises. There might also be guaranteed minimum standards of public services, in return for the taxes they receive.

It should also be possible to change the rules of democracy in Parliament so that Select Committees, locally, as well as nationally, have greater power of scrutiny over decision-makers, and the ability to draw more thoroughly on the advice and evidence of regulators, auditors and inspectors. The rules of democratic accountability for public bodies should be strengthened to require them to report on their good practice as well as their good accounting.

And there may be a need to amend the rules of democracy that apply to all of us. As members of communities, we already have to obey the law and pay taxes; in future, we may need to consider a similar obligation to vote, and to contribute time and money to our own communities, so we share responsibility for their improvement.

If the rules of democracy change in these or similar ways, we would have more say over decisions that impact on our lives, politicians would become more accountable for their words and businesses for their actions, and public services would improve faster by learning from others.

Changing rules

These long-term goals could be dismissed as lacking realism or pragmatism. But others have speculated before about better ways to govern their communities. Around 375 BC, Plato proposed in his *Republic* some rules for hypothetical cities and a utopian city-state ruled by a philosopher-king. In 1787, Alexander Hamilton and James Madison wrote in their *Federalist papers* how the future United States should be governed, including by adopting a written constitution. Max Weber, in his *Economy and society* of 1922, described ideal types of public administration, including the most efficient and rational way of organising the provision of communal services.[5] These authors and many others have identified problems with the governance of their own communities and tried to suggest ways of ensuring that better decisions are made for everyone's benefit. After the Industrial Revolution 200 years ago, many changes were made to the rules of democracy: fairer constituencies were established; secret ballots were introduced; working men and then women got the vote; and election spending was regulated. None of these changes was quickly achieved.

Making changes to the rules that govern communities is never easy. Some of the changes proposed here are modest: public services could share good practice; parliamentary Select Committees could receive regular reports from regulators and have more power to hold politicians to account. Other suggestions, such as for a global parliament, a personal online tax account, compulsory voting and new laws to keep politicians honest, are more ambitious. Implementing them will cost money, and some will be hard to enforce. Others may require a paradigm shift in the way we think about our communities and how they are governed.[6]

Implementing any proposals to change the rules of democracy will take time. It requires many people in many communities to recognise that change is necessary, and then to say so, debating with others exactly what form the changes might take. There is opposition to overcome, both to the principle of change and then to the details. Politicians need to agree to new rules that may limit their power and make them more accountable to those they represent. None of this is straightforward, and it may not be possible.

But this book argues that some change needs to happen. Whether through the suggestions here or others, the challenges to collective decision-making that have been presented by the Global Technological Revolution will need to be met. In democracies, this means that the rules of the game of democracy itself may need to evolve, as they have done before.

Good decision-making comes at a cost. Businesses understand this. Decision-making in commercial organisations is neither instant nor free. It involves people getting together and spending time researching and debating what to do. This costs time and money. But the process is considered worthwhile because good decisions can lead to profits and bad decisions to ruin.

Decision-making in a democracy is no different. We choose politicians to represent us and then send them to the place where decisions are made. We want them to consult us regularly and help to resolve our problems. We do not want them to rush important decisions, except in a crisis. Good decision-making in a democracy involves talking, and that takes time. Talking is a good way to resolve differences and to find solutions to difficult problems. It also costs money. And, as in business, the democratic decision-making process is worthwhile because good decisions can lead to safe, healthy, successful communities and bad decisions may lead to poverty, disease and war.

Decision-making in undemocratic countries also costs money. Factions and interests need to be reconciled and paid off. And there is an increased risk of corruption, bad business deals and economic mismanagement. Authoritarian decisions may not be cheaper and are likely to be worse. Democracy is worth the money.

Enforcing the rules of democracy

If new rules of democracy are ever agreed, they will need to be enforced. We want politicians and public services to play by the rules so that we have greater confidence in those we choose to represent us and to make decisions on our behalf. The rules must be enforced fairly and independently so that politicians and other decision-makers can be accountable to us.

In games such as football and other sports, rules, once agreed, are enforced by referees. In the game of democracy, the rules are enforced by judges and regulators. This may make a final new rule of democracy necessary:

> Independent, accountable regulators, as well as an independent judiciary, should enforce the rules of democracy as they apply to politicians, public bodies and us.

Independent, accountable regulators of public services, and of democracy itself, alongside an independent judiciary, give communities confidence that those making decisions are playing by the rules and can be held to account for their words and actions. Judges, including in Election Courts, can oversee the laws of democracy. The regulators of public services in the UK include the Care Quality Commission, the Environment Agency, the Office of Rail and Road, the Equality and Human Rights Commission, the Independent Office of Police Conduct, and many others. The regulators of democracy include the

National Audit Office, the Electoral Commission, the Boundary Commissions and the Independent Parliamentary Standards Authority. They help to ensure the integrity of democracy itself.

Regulators are not much liked. The same goes with being a referee. They apply the rules, and no one likes rules being applied to them. Regulators are sometimes criticised for being too hard or too soft, for putting in place too many restrictions, or for having too few, for failing to allow innovation, or for not protecting the vulnerable. Their decisions may be contentious or unpopular. For regulators to do their jobs well, they must have deep expertise and sound judgement.

It helps their effectiveness if regulators are independent. Independent regulation allows us to trust expert watchdogs to keep an eye on politicians and public services on our behalf. The regulators of democracy can then make sure, without fear or favour, that politicians are elected fairly and that they behave honestly in their work on our behalf.

But regulators should also be accountable, through politicians to voters. They must work transparently, consulting on the rules they set, and explaining their decisions. They must involve interested parties, including the producers and consumers of the public services being regulated. They must explain their work clearly so we can understand their findings, including how safe our food is or how good our schools are. Their decisions must be subject to scrutiny and challenge. This means regulators being held to account by politicians in parliamentary Select Committees. And we should be able to take regulators to court, including through a judicial review, if we think they have made the wrong decisions.

Most people in a community, including most businesses and most politicians, play by the rules. When they do, regulation is often invisible, like a referee who goes unnoticed during a good sporting match or game of football. But the regulators are there, as the community's watchdogs, to help prevent things going wrong, and to take action if they do. The referees of democracy similarly keep guard of the rules on our behalf.

Professional regulators who are independent and accountable can help to ensure that politicians and public services play by the rules, including any future changed rules of democracy. New rules, well refereed and applied fairly, can help to overcome the challenges presented by the Global Technological Revolution and increase confidence in democracy as an effective way to make difficult decisions on behalf of communities.

Concluding words

Politicians of all parties do a difficult job, often under intense pressure and public scrutiny, to lead and improve their communities. Senior decision-makers in government and public services work hard to tackle and resolve complex social and economic problems. Charities, academics and researchers, and many others, all contribute to understanding and addressing specific problems that reduce individual and community wellbeing. This book supports their work by suggesting how future communities may choose to govern themselves more democratically and more accountably.

Any actual changes to the rules of democracy will not come from a book, but from action. Politicians will ultimately decide whether to change the rules of the game of democracy, but they will only do so, rightly, in response to the expressed demands of their electorate. That is why voting makes a difference. And we can make a tangible difference in more immediate ways by discussing with others how to improve our communities and by volunteering to make improvements happen. Every positive action, even picking up a plastic bottle, makes a difference. Communities do not change without individual action.

The rules of democracy may not evolve in line with the suggestions here, because all changes to the rules must be determined by elected politicians in response to the wishes of their communities. But the rules need to evolve. The advent of the Global Technological Revolution has made our governance status quo increasingly untenable. Decisions that impact on our lives are too often made behind closed doors by the leaders of powerful, rich countries, particularly China, the US and Russia, by the unaccountable bosses of global tech and logistics firms, and by invisible bureaucrats. We know too little about how our taxes are raised or spent. A few politicians can lie and cheat to win power, and there is little to prevent them.

And public services are struggling to cope with demand and restricted budgets.

Instead, there may be ways to change the rules so that communities can improve. We can each get more involved in our communities too, and help our elected politicians to make difficult decisions on our behalf and in our best interests, while holding them to account. And we may need to have a better, more democratic way of participating in global decisions that impact on our lives, whether we live in Africa, Asia or the Americas.

Changing the rules of democracy is not easy. It involves changing how our communities are governed, including who makes decisions, how and when. But democracy has evolved before, and it can again to respond to the challenges of the Global Technological Revolution. Whether and how it does is now up to us.

Appendix:
The rules of democracy

These rules summarise democracy as it currently operates:

1. People are born with equal rights, including to freedom and safety from harm.
2. People naturally form communities of various sizes, including families, tribes, towns and nations. These communities provide the people who are in them with benefits, including security, identity and health.
3. People are required to cede some of their rights, such as to unfettered freedom, to their communities, in return for the benefits, such as security.
4. These benefits cost the communities money and effort to provide. Communities must raise the money to provide the benefits, mostly by imposing taxes on the people from their own community.
5. People in each community must decide which benefits their community should provide to its members, as well as how money should be raised to fund these benefits. Rather than allow an absolute ruler or small elite to make these decisions in their own narrow interests, people in democratic communities have developed ways to choose representatives to make decisions on behalf of the community as a whole. These representatives are the politicians elected in democracies.
6. The decisions themselves become codified into rules, such as laws and accepted practice. People in the communities are required to adhere to these rules on penalty of enforceable sanctions. The laws and accepted practice change over time in line with the decisions made by elected representatives on behalf of the communities they represent.

7. Elected representatives establish institutions to provide the benefits to the community and to raise the money to fund them, in line with their decisions and the rules they have created. These institutions include public services and all other services funded through taxation.

Future rules of democracy may include:

8. Elected representatives should exist at every level where decisions are taken that impact on the represented communities, whether these decisions are taken locally, nationally or internationally (see Chapter 3).
9. How taxes are raised and spent should be wholly transparent to those paying the taxes, with sufficient tax-raising powers at every democratic level where politicians make spending decisions on behalf of their communities (see Chapter 4).
10. Politicians must adhere to the rule of law and the rules of democracy, including by being accountable for their words, their actions and the impact of their decisions (see Chapter 5).
11. All organisations receiving taxes must be accountable both for how they spend public money and for sharing their learning and good practice (see Chapter 6).
12. Each member of a community must adhere to the rule of law and the rules of democracy, including by paying taxes, voting and contributing time and money to their community (see Chapter 7).
13. Independent, accountable regulators, as well as an independent judiciary, should enforce the rules of democracy as they apply to politicians, public bodies and us (see the Conclusion).

Notes

Introduction

[1] See, respectively, James Dale Davidson and William Rees-Mogg (1997) *The sovereign individual: Mastering the transition to the information age*, New York: Simon & Schuster, and Jamie Susskind (2018) *Future politics: Living together in a world transformed by tech*, Oxford: Oxford University Press. Andrew Blick (2021) *Electrified democracy: The internet and the United Kingdom Parliament in history*, Cambridge: Cambridge University Press, also discusses the actual and potential impact of the internet on democracy.

[2] The Hansard Society's 2017 *Audit of political engagement* found that only 30 per cent of respondents in the UK were satisfied with how Parliament works. And voter turnout around the world has declined: see Thomas Edward Flores and Ifran Nooruddin (2016) *Elections in hard times: Building stronger democracies in the 21st century*, Cambridge: Cambridge University Press. See also Roberto Stefan Foa and Yascha Mounk (2016) 'The danger of deconsolidation: The democratic disconnect', *Journal of Democracy*, 27(3), July, 5–17. A comprehensive account of the current threats to democracy is given in Steven Levitsky and Daniel Ziblatt's (2018) *How democracies die: What history reveals about our future*, London: Penguin. The problems of disenchantment with politics are also well covered by Gerry Stoker (2006) *Why politics matters: Making democracy work*, London: Bloomsbury, and by Colin Hay (2007) *Why we hate politics*, Cambridge: Polity Press.

[3] This separation of power between those who propose rules (that is, our political leaders in the executive government), those who agree the rules (that is, the politicians of the legislature) and those who enforce the rules (that is, the judiciary) has been articulated since Charles de Montesquieu wrote *The spirit of the laws* in 1748. It is core to the American constitution of 1787, and has been at the heart of good democratic governance since.

[4] See Bronwen Morgan and Karen Yeung (2003) *An introduction to law and regulation: Text and materials*, Cambridge: Cambridge University Press.

[5] Tower Hamlets Council later apologised and waived the fine (reported by the BBC and other media, 21 July 2017, see www.bbc.co.uk/news/uk-england-london-40679075).

[6] Among many examples, US Senator Harrison A. Williams was convicted of bribery and conspiracy in 1982, Australian MP Steve Irons was convicted of drink driving in 2015, and Japanese Cabinet members Isshu Sugawara

and Katsuyuki Kawai resigned following allegations of bribery and vote-buying in October 2019.

7 Bruce Ackerman (2000) 'The new separation of powers', *Harvard Law Review*, 113(3), 633–729, p 718. See also Robert Hazell (1997) 'Constitutional watchdogs', *Delivering constitutional reform: The Constitution Unit's collected briefings* (pp 83–93), London: Constitution Unit, UCL; and James Spigelman (2004) 'The integrity branch of government', *Australian Law Journal*, 78(11), 724.

Chapter 1

1 Daron Acemoglu and James Robinson (2013) *Why nations fail: The origins of power, prosperity and poverty*, London: Profile Books; Max Weber (2019) *Economy and society: A new translation* (edited and transcribed by Keith Tribe), Cambridge, MA: Harvard University Press.

2 John G. Matsusaka (2005) 'Direct democracy works', *Journal of Economic Perspectives*, 19(2), 185–206. See also Ian Budge (2006) 'Direct and representative democracy: Are they necessarily opposed?', *Representation*, 42, 1–12.

3 Sarah Repucci and Amy Slipowitz (2021) *Freedom in the world 2021: Democracy under siege*, Washington, DC: Freedom House. The US and UK statistics come respectively from Lee Drutman, Joe Goldman and Larry Diamond (2020) 'Democracy maybe: Attitudes on authoritarianism in America', Democracy Fund Voter Study Group, June, and from the Hansard Society (2019) *Audit of political engagement 16: The 2019 report*. Yascha Mounk (2018) *The people vs democracy: Why our freedom is in danger and how to save it*, Cambridge, MA: Harvard University Press, also shows how support for democracy can erode.

4 Dan Bang and Chris D. Frith (2017) 'Making better decisions in groups', *Royal Society for Open Science*, 4(8), 170–93. See also Frederick C. Miner (1984) 'Group versus individual decision making: An investigation of performance measures, decision strategies, and process losses/gains', *Organizational Behavior and Human Performance*, 33, 112–24.

5 The evidence here comes from Florence Jaumotte, Ksenia Koloskova and Sweta Saxena (2016) 'Impact of migration on income levels in advanced economies', *Spillover Notes*, International Monetary Fund, October; Said Adejumobi (2000) 'Between democracy and development in Africa: What are the missing links?', Conference Paper, Paris: World Bank; Augustin Kwasi Fosu (2020) *Democracy and development in Africa*, University of Pretoria Working Paper; Alex Nowrasteh and Benjamin Powell (2020) *Wretched refuse? The political economy of immigration and institutions*, Cambridge: Cambridge University Press; and *The Economist* (2020) 'COVID-19 and democracy', 6 June, p 81.

Chapter 2

1   See Eskarne Arregui Pabollet, Margherita Bacigalupo, Federico Biagi, Marcelino Cabrera Giraldez, Francesca Caena, Jonatan Castaño Muñoz, J. et al (2019) *The changing nature of work and skills in the digital age*, EU Science Hub, Luxembourg: Publications Office of the European Union; and Peadar Kirby (2005) *Vulnerability and violence: The impact of globalisation*, London: Pluto Press.

2   Respectively, see US Senate Intelligence Committee (2017) 'Assessing Russian activities and intentions in recent US elections', 6 January; UK Parliament, Digital, Culture, Media and Sport Committee (2018) *Disinformation and 'fake news': Interim report*, Fifth Report of Session 2017–19, HC 363, 29 July, para 41; and Vidya Narayanan, Bence Kollanyi, Ruchi Hajela, Ankita Barthwal, Nahema Marchal and Philip N. Howard (2019) 'News and information over Facebook and WhatsApp during the Indian election campaign', Data memo from the Project on Computational Propaganda, University of Oxford, 13 May.

3   A comprehensive account of the problem can be found in the UK Parliament's Joint Committee on Human Rights (2019) report, *Democracy, freedom of expression and freedom of association: Threats to MPs*, HC 37, HL 5, 18 October. See also the Committee on Standards in Public Life's (2017) report, *Intimidation in public life*.

4   See, for example, David Wainwright and Michael Calnan (2002) *Work stress: The making of a modern epidemic*, Maidenhead: Open University Press.

5   Figures are from Brian Bell and John van Reenan (2013) 'Bankers and their bonuses', *The Economic Journal*, 124, February; and Alan S. Blinder (2016) *After the music stopped: The financial crisis, the response, and the work ahead*, London: Penguin.

6   The estimates come from David S. Wall (2007) *Cybercrime: The transformation of crime in the Information Age*, Cambridge: Polity Press.

7   Between 2012 and 2016, Thomas Reid successfully prevented a planned new US$8 billion facility at Intel's factory in County Kildare, Ireland. His story was made into a documentary film, *The lonely battle of Thomas Reid*, in 2017.

8   Mark Bovens is the authority on democratic accountability. See his (2007) 'Analysing and assessing accountability: A conceptual framework', *European Law Journal*, 13(4), July, 447–68, and also (2010) 'Two concepts of accountability: Accountability as a virtue and as a mechanism', *West European Politics*, 33(5), 946–67.

9   The figures here come from the following reports – mean response rate for Category 2 (emergency) calls in the UK was 28 minutes in December 2019, with 90 per cent of calls answered within an hour: Nuffield Trust (2020) 'Ambulance response times', 1 May; National Audit Office (2016) *The quality of service for personal taxpayers*, HC 17 2016-17, 25 May. An annual survey of 901 UK GP practices found an average wait of 14.8 days for the first GP appointment: *Pulse Today*, 19 August 2019.

[10] NatCen Social Research, British Social Attitudes 2017 survey, reported in Ruth Robertson and John Appleby (2018) *Public satisfaction with the NHS and social care in 2017*, London: The King's Fund, 28 February. See also Transport Focus (2019) *National Rail passenger survey*, 29 January.

[11] Among the enormous literature on the history and impact of the Industrial Revolution, a good place to start is Pat Hudson (1992) *The Industrial Revolution*, London: Edward Arnold.

[12] These and other examples are provided in Eric J. Evans (1994) *The Great Reform Act of 1832*, Lancaster Pamphlets, London: Routledge; and John Keane (2009) *The life and death of democracy*, New York: Simon & Schuster, p 503.

[13] For full background on the Beveridge report and its impact, see Nicholas Timmins (2017) *The five giants: A biography of the welfare state*, London: William Collins.

[14] Institute for Fiscal Studies (2015) *Recent cuts to public spending*, 1 October, drawing on HM Treasury (2015) *Public expenditure statistical analyses 2015*.

[15] See Vito Tanzi and Ludger Schuknecht (2000) *Public spending in the twentieth century: A global perspective*, Cambridge: Cambridge University Press.

[16] Esteban Ortiz-Ospina (2016) 'Government spending', OurWorldInData. org (https://ourworldindata.org/government-spending), drawing on Andrea De Mauro, Marco Greco and Michele Grimaldi (2015) 'What is big data? A consensual definition and a review of key research topics, *AIP Conference Proceedings*, 1644(97) (https://aip.scitation.org/doi/abs/10.1063/1.4907823).

[17] Fiscal Affairs Department data, based on Paolo Mauro, Rafael Romeu, Ariel Binder and Asad Zaman (2015) 'A modern history of fiscal prudence and profligacy', *Journal of Monetary Economics*, 76, 55–70 (see www.imf.org/external/datamapper/datasets/FPP/1).

[18] The statistics here are all published by the Office of Rail and Road (https://dataportal.orr.gov.uk).

[19] Thomas Jefferson penned the phrase 'all men are created equal' in the US Declaration of Independence in 1776. Mary Wollstonecraft called for equality between men and women in her (1792) *A vindication of the rights of women*.

Chapter 3

[1] A good overview in the context of the EU is given by Andreas Føllesdal (1998) 'Survey article: Subsidiarity', *The Journal of Political Philosophy*, 6(2), 190–218.

[2] This is a simplistic characterisation. For a good starting point on the wealth of research in this area, see Diane K. Denis and John J. McConnell (2009) *International corporate governance*, Cambridge: Cambridge University Press.

[3] See Gerald M. Weinberg (1975) *An introduction to general systems thinking*, New York: Dorset House; and Michael C. Jackson (2019) *Critical systems thinking and the management of complexity*, Hoboken, NJ: John Wiley & Sons.

4   From the large literature on global governance, see, for example, Raimo Väyrynen (ed) (1999) *Globalization and global governance*, Lanham, MD: Rowman & Littlefield; and John Bew (2015) *Realpolitik: A history*, Oxford: Oxford University Press.

5   *The Economist* (2021) 'Looking for someone to blame', 6 February.

6   UK Parliament, House of Commons Library (2020) *A guide to the EU budget*, 25 September; European Union (2020) *Statistical Factsheet: Food, farming, fisheries*, June.

7   A desire for a parliamentary assembly was discussed at the founding of the League of Nations in 1919 and more recently by Jürgen Habermas (1999) *The inclusion of the other: Studies in political theory*, Cambridge: Polity Press, and William Scheuerman (2011) *The realist case for global reform*, Cambridge: Polity Press, who consider a world parliament logically necessary. Jo Leinen and Andreas Bummel (2018) *A world parliament: Governance and democracy in the 21st century*, Berlin: Democracy Without Borders, provide a history of the proposal and discuss its current relevance and implementation. See also Maja Brauer and Andreas Bummel (2020) *A United Nations parliamentary assembly*, Berlin: Democracy Without Borders.

8   Possible approaches are outlined in Joseph Schwartzberg (2012) *Creating a world parliamentary assembly: An evolutionary journey*, Berlin: Committee for a Democratic UN.

9   Thomas Piketty (2014) *Capital in the twenty-first century*, Cambridge: Cambridge University Press, argues for a progressive global tax on capital (p 515). Presidents Jacques Chirac and Ernesto Zedillo, of France and Mexico respectively, suggested at a UN conference in Monterrey (18–22 March 2002) that a global tax might apply to international currency transactions and CO_2 emissions.

10 The figures come from a survey of 2,000 people conducted by the TSB Bank and reported on 4 January 2016 (www.tsb.co.uk/news-releases/britain-is-a-nation-of-homebirds) and from Gillian B. White (2015) 'Staying close to home, no matter what', *The Atlantic*, 18 March 2015 (www.theatlantic.com/business/archive/2015/03/staying-close-to-home-no-matter-what/387736). See also David K. Ihrke and Carol S. Faber (2012) *Geographical mobility: 2005 to 2010*, Washington, DC: United States Census Bureau, December.

11 Proponents of greater devolution of power include Labour MP Alan Milburn in (2004) 'Localism: The need for a new settlement', London: Demos; Conservative MP James Morris in (2010) 'Localism and decentralisation', Conservative Home; and UK think tanks Localis and New Local.

12 Office for Budget Responsibility (2020) *Locally financed expenditure*, 15 September; Peter Locher and Ernst Blumenstein (2002) *System des schweizerischen Steuerrechts* (6th edn), Zürich: Verlag Schulthess. For an introduction to historical issues relevant to local taxation, see Allan McConnell (2012) *The politics and policy of local taxation in Britain*, Cambridge: Cambridge Academic.

[13] See Local Government Association (2018) *National census of local authority councillors 2018*. In many places, local democracy is for the retired or under-employed. In 2018, the average age of elected local politicians in the UK was 59, with 45 per cent already retired and only 15 per cent under 45. Some 63 per cent were men and 96 per cent described their ethnicity as 'white'.

[14] Daniel Bell (1987) 'The world and the United States in 2013', *Daedalus*, 116(3), Summer, 1–31, pp 13–14.

[15] For an introduction to the history and philosophy of identity issues, see Harold Noonan (2019) *Personal identity* (3rd edn), Abingdon: Routledge. For the impact of the internet on identity, see Andoni Alonso and Pedro Oiarzabal (eds) (2010) *Diasporas in the new media age: Identity, politics, and community*, Reno, NV: University of Nevada Press.

Chapter 4

[1] The history of tax is admirably charted by Charles Adams (1992) *For good and evil: The impact of taxes on the course of civilization*, Seattle, WA: Madison Books.

[2] For the evidence behind these figures, see Matthew Gardner, Steve Wamhoff, Mary Martellota and Lorena Roque (2019) 'Corporate tax avoidance remains rampant', Institute on Taxation and Economic Policy, 11 April; Jim Corkery, Jay Forder, Dan Svantesson and Enrico Mercuri (2013) 'Taxes, the internet and the digital economy', *Revenue Law Journal*, 23(1), 1 January; and Charles Duhigg and David Kocieniewski (2012) 'How Apple sidesteps billions in global taxes', *The New York Times*, 28 April. See also Katarzyna Habu (2016) 'How aggressive are foreign multinational companies in avoiding corporation tax?', Institute of Fiscal Studies, 3 October; and Erik Sherman (2019) 'Big tech companies used legal loopholes to avoid over $100 billion in taxes', *Fortune Magazine*, 6 December.

[3] Erin Duffin (2020) 'Total lobbying spending US 1998–2019', Statista, 4 March.

[4] James Andreoni, Brian Erard and Jonathan Feinstein (1998) 'Tax compliance', *Journal of Economic Literature*, 36(2), June.

[5] For the evidence to support these numbers, see Ceyhun Elgin and Oguz Oztunali (2012) *Shadow economies around the world: Model-based estimates*, Boğaziçi University Department of Economics Working Paper, 10 May; Annette Alstadsaeter, Niels Johannesen and Gabriel Zucman (2017) 'Tax evasion and inequality', *American Economic Review*, 109(6), June; and Ernesto Crivelli, Ruud A. de Mooij and Michael Keen (2016) *Base erosion, profit shifting and developing countries*, International Monetary Fund Working Papers, 15/118. In addition, in Alex Cobham, Javier Garcia-Bernardo, Miroslav Palansky and Mark Bou Mansour (2020) *The state of tax justice*, Bristol: Tax Justice Network, 20 November, they estimate that, across the world, £427 billion is lost each year to tax havens that might otherwise fund public services.

6   For a comparison of international tax regimes, see Tax Foundation (2020) *2020 International Tax Competitiveness Index* (https://tax-competition.org).

7   See Simon James, Adrian Sawyer and Tamer Budak (2015) *The complexity of tax simplification: Experiences from around the world*, Basingstoke: Palgrave Macmillan; Tracey Bowler (2014) *The Office of Tax Simplification: Looking back and looking forward*, Discussion Paper No 11, Tax Law Review Committee, London: Institute for Fiscal Studies; and HM Revenue and Customs (2020) *Measuring tax gaps: Tax gap estimates for 2018–19*, 9 July.

8   Some of the arguments for greater tax transparency are outlined in Lynn Oats and Penelope Tuck (2019) 'Corporate tax avoidance: Is tax transparency the solution?', *Accounting and Business Research*, 49(5), 565–83. The debate currently focuses more on requiring firms to publish their tax strategies than on more comprehensive ways of bringing transparency to taxation and public expenditure for everyone.

9   The value of public audit is assessed in Jeremy Lonsdale, Peter Wilkins and Tom Ling (eds) (2011) *Performance auditing: Contributing to accountability in democratic government*, Cheltenham: Edward Elgar, and questioned in Åge Johnsen (2019) 'Public sector audit in contemporary society: A short review and introduction', *Financial Accountability and Management*, 35(2), 127–9. See also Kevin Page (2014) *External review of the Office for Budget Responsibility*, London: HMSO, which concluded that the OBR has reduced perceptions of bias due to the calibre of its staff and its methodology.

10 The figures in this section come from Thomas Pope and Tom Waters (2016) *A survey of the UK tax system*, Briefing Note BN09, London: Institute for Fiscal Studies, November, and Institute for Fiscal Studies (2015) *Total public spending*, 28 September, as well as from the OBR's monthly *Economic and Fiscal Outlook Profiles* (including for November 2020, published on 22 December 2020).

11 From 1 April 2021, the TV licence fee cost £159 for every household. This is not a tax, but it raises money to fund a public service, and the sums raised are not automatically and directly paid to the BBC (that is, it is not hypothecated), and so it is included here.

12 Vehicle tax rates for 2020–21 ranged from £0 for cars that do not emit CO_2 to £2,175 for those that emit over 255g/km (www.gov.uk/vehicle-tax-rate-tables).

13 Office for National Statistics (2017) *Public sector finances, UK: April 2017*, 23 May.

14 World Bank (2021) 'Net ODA received (% of GNI)' (https://data.worldbank.org/indicator/DT.ODA.ODAT.GN.ZS).

15 Figures come primarily from the OECD Tax Database (see www.oecd.org/tax/tax-policy/tax-database).

16 Throughout her political career, former Prime Minister Margaret Thatcher successfully used the analogy to compare the national budget with domestic finances, but Roger Farmer and Pawel Zabcyck argue persuasively in (2018) *The household fallacy*, CEPR Discussion Papers, London: Centre for

Economic Policy Research, March, that governments, unlike households, can create their own money to repay debt.

17   National Audit Office (2020) *Whole of government accounts: Year ended 31 March 2019*, London: HMSO, 21 July, p 17. The Institute for Fiscal Studies has also tried to collate data on public spending, as in Carl Emmerson and Christine Frayne (2005) *Public spending*, IFS 2005 Election Briefing Note No 2.

18   See https://tax.demos.co.uk

19   The accounts of all UK government departments were reviewed from 2006–07, after a few years of relative economic stability and before the financial crisis of 2008 and the austerity that followed. Various assumptions were made to simplify the presentation of the figures.

20   This is created separately for each employment, and does not give an overall picture of taxes paid.

21   According to the industry body UK Finance, just 23 per cent of purchases in 2019 involved cash, with card payments accounting for 51 per cent of transactions (*UK Payment Markets*, June 2020). By November 2020, 36 per cent of purchases were being made online: Office for National Statistics (2020) *Retail Sales Index*, 18 December.

22   The Mirrlees Review of the UK tax system concluded that it was ripe for simplification. See James Mirrlees (2011) *Tax by design*, London: Institute for Fiscal Studies, 13 September.

23   Cait Poynor Lamberton, Jan-Emmanuel De Neve and Michael Norton (2014) *Eliciting taxpayer preferences increases tax compliance*, SSRN, 24 April.

24   Ana Luisa Neve, Lisa Freise, Liliana Laranjo, Alexander Carter, Ara Darzi and Erik Mayer (2020) 'Impact of providing patients access to electronic health records on quality and safety of care: A systematic review and meta-analysis', *BMJ Quality & Safety*, 29(12).

Chapter 5

1   Jane Roberts (2017) *Losing political office*, Basingstoke: Palgrave Macmillan.

2   For a classic study of how politicians seek to insulate themselves from electoral tests, see John Ely (1980) *Democracy and distrust: A theory of judicial review*, Cambridge, MA: Harvard University Press.

3   Nicholas Stephanopoulos (2018) 'The causes and consequences of gerrymandering', *William and Mary Law Review*, 59(5), 2115–58.

4   UK election rules could nonetheless be strengthened. See Electoral Commission (2020) *Reforming electoral law*, 3 November. The Committee on Standards in Public Life also recommended changes to reduce political parties' reliance on large donations in their (2011) *Political party finance: Ending the big donor culture*, 1 November. The US does not have an independent Electoral Commission. This perhaps made it easier for former President Donald Trump to inaccurately claim that he had lost the 2020 presidential election, albeit that the rules of democracy in the US were ultimately upheld by state legislatures, the US Supreme Court and by then Vice-President Mike Pence.

5   Max Rosenthal (2011) 'Texans allowed to show gun permits but not student IDs at voting booth', *Huffington Post*, 16 November.

6   Following the 2015 General Election, the Electoral Commission referred Craig Mackinlay MP to the police, alleging electoral fraud. In January 2019 he was found 'not guilty' in court. In 2017, IPSA asked the police to investigate whether Chris Davies MP had committed false accounting. In March 2019 he was found 'guilty' in court.

7   The seven principles of public life are, selflessness, integrity, objectivity, accountability, openness, honesty and leadership. They are also known as the 'Nolan Principles', after Michael Nolan, the first chair of the Committee on Standards in Public Life, which is responsible for advising on ethical standards in public life.

8   Following the November 2020 US presidential election, some social media platforms temporarily or permanently closed the account of Donald Trump, allegedly to stop him inciting violence. This re-emphasised ongoing questions about the editorial responsibilities of global technology firms, and how they themselves are accountable for their decisions to allow or ban the publication of users' content.

9   Section 3 of the Advertising Standards Authority's 'Code of Non-Broadcast Advertising and Direct and Promotional Marketing' (www.asa.org.uk/ codes-and-rulings/advertising-codes/non-broadcast-code.html).

10   The EU's 'Unfair Commercial Practices Directive 2005', as amended in 2019 (https://ec.europa.eu/info/law/law-topic/consumer-protection-law/ unfair-commercial-practices-law/unfair-commercial-practices-directive_ en).

11   Perjury is defined in the Perjury Act of 1911. Misconduct in public office is a common law offence that has existed in the UK for hundreds of years. The Law Commission has recommended its overhaul. See Law Commission (2020) *Misconduct in public office*, LC 397, HC 1027, London: HMSO, 3 December. See also Richard Rampton, Heather Rogers, Timothy Atkinson and Aidan Eardley (eds) (2020) *Duncan and Neill on defamation* (5th edn), LexisNexis; and Patrick Milmo, W.V.H. Rogers and Richard Parkes (eds) (2003) *Gatley on libel and slander* (10th edn), London: Sweet & Maxwell.

12   The relevant legislation on hate speech includes Parts 3, 3A and 4 of the Public Order Act 1986, as amended by subsequent legislation: 'A person who uses threatening, abusive or insulting words or behaviour, or displays any written material which is threatening, abusive or insulting, is guilty of an offence'.

13   See, respectively, UK High Court of Justice, Queen's Bench, Election Court [2010] EWHC 2702 (QB), 5 November 2010; and UK High Court of Justice, Queen's Bench, Election Court [2015] EWHC 1215 (QB), 23 April 2015.

14   As in Section 3 of the Advertising Standards Authority's Code, referred to in note 9 above.

15 This is where members of a community debate or deliberate on current issues, so decisions made by politicians are informed by a wider range of views. See John Parkinson and Jane Mansbridge (eds) (2012) *Deliberative systems: Deliberative democracy at the large scale*, Cambridge: Cambridge University Press. Andrew Blick (2021) *Electrified democracy: The internet and the United Kingdom Parliament in history*, Cambridge: Cambridge University Press also discusses how technology can facilitate community decision-making.

16 See Yanina Welp and Laurence Whitehead (eds) (2020) *The politics of recall elections*, Basingstoke: Palgrave Macmillan. Fiona Onasanya, MP for Peterborough, was recalled in March 2019 after being convicted of lying to the police in relation to a speeding offence. Chris Davies, MP for Brecon and Radnorshire, was recalled in May 2019 after being convicted of submitting a false expense claim. Ms Onasanya did not stand at the subsequent election. Mr Davies did, and lost. In August 2018, Ian Paisley Jr, MP for North Antrim, was at risk for recall following his suspension from Parliament for accepting hospitality from Sri Lanka and not declaring it. The recall petition was not signed by the required 10 per cent of voters, so an election was not called in his constituency.

17 Marc Geddes (2020) *Dramas at Westminster: Select Committees and the quest for accountability*, Manchester: Manchester University Press; Hannah White (2015) *Select Committees under scrutiny: The impact of parliamentary committee inquiries on government*, London: Institute for Government. See also Lucy Atkinson (2017) *House of Commons Select Committees and the UK Constitution*, London: The Constitution Society. The 40 per cent figure comes from Meghan Benton and Meg Russell (2013) 'Assessing the impact of parliamentary oversight committees: The Select Committees in the British House of Commons', *Parliamentary Affairs*, 66(4), October, 772–97.

18 On 25 April 2018, Amber Rudd told MPs that the government had no targets to remove immigrants. It had, and Ms Rudd resigned. An internal report later found that Home Office officials had given her incorrect information: Home Office (2018) *Sir Alex Allan review: Executive summary*, London (www.gov.uk/government/publications/sir-alex-allan-review-executive-summary).

19 Dilma Rousseff was impeached on 31 August 2016 for breaking budget laws. Park Geun-hye was impeached on 9 December 2016 for abuse of power, bribery, coercion and leaking secrets. Donald Trump was impeached twice: on 18 December 2019 for abuse of power and on 13 January 2021 for inciting an insurrection. Spain's Prime Minister Mariano Rajoy lost office after a vote of no confidence on 1 June 2018. Sweden's Prime Minister Stefan Löfven lost a vote of no confidence in September 2018 but survived to lead a new coalition government. Pakistan's Prime Minister Benazir Bhutto defeated a vote of no confidence in November 1989.

20 Marc Geddes (2020) *Dramas at Westminster: Select Committees and the quest for accountability*, Manchester: Manchester University Press describes MPs on Select Committees as having performance roles such as 'specialist',

'lone wolf', 'constituency champion', 'party helper', 'learner' or 'absentee'. Oonagh Gray (2012) *Individual ministerial accountability*, House of Commons Research Paper 06467, 8 November, also notes that other parliamentary conventions and rulebooks, including the Osmotherly Rules and the Cabinet Manual, need updating to improve accountability.

21 National Audit Office (2019) *Transforming rehabilitation: Progress review*, 1 March concluded that Mr Grayling's Ministry had 'rushed implementation [and] introduced significant risks. ... There is little evidence of hoped-for innovation and many of the early operational issues ... persist. [The probation reform] has achieved poor value for money ... the Ministry will pay at least £467 million more than was required.'

22 As in US law, protecting those in official positions who make 'reasonable but mistaken judgments'. See *Harlow v Fitzgerald*, 457 US 800 (1982).

23 See J.C. Holt (2015) *Magna Carta*, Cambridge: Cambridge University Press and John Keane (2009) *The life and death of democracy*, New York: Simon & Schuster, pp 173–8 on the 1188 Cortes de León, where King Alfonso IX was forced to promise that, from then on, he would accept advice from his bishops, nobles and 'good men' of the town on matters of war and peace treaties. Like the Magna Carta a generation later in England, this broke the tradition of unquestioning loyalty to the sovereign.

24 *British Medical Journal* (2017) 'UK has fewer doctors per person than most other OECD countries', 357, 2940, 20 June.

25 On 18 July 2020, UN Secretary-General António Guterres said: 'A changing world requires a new generation of social protection policies with new safety nets including ... establishing minimum levels of social protection. ... Taxation has also a role In the New Social Contract. Everyone – individuals and corporations – must pay their fair share' (Nelson Mandela Annual Lecture, 2020, 'Tackling inequality: A new social contract for a new era'). See also UNDP (2016) *Engaged societies, responsive states: The social contract in situations of conflict and fragility*, April; and the OECD discussion forum (www.oecd-forum.org/badges/634-new-societal-contract).

Chapter 6

1 In the decade from 2009 to 2019, across the 309,000 people who responded to the annual surveys of the UK civil service, only two-thirds received regular performance feedback, and 60 per cent or more said that poor performance was not dealt with effectively. See Cabinet Office (2020) *People survey: Civil service benchmark scores 2009 to 2019*. Ways to improve public sector management are outlined in: Marcial Bóo and Alexander Stevenson (2015) *The public sector fox: Twelve ways to become a brilliant public sector manager*, Kibworth Beauchamp: Matador.

2 Frank Verbeeten (2008) 'Performance management practices in public sector organizations: Impact on performance', *Accounting, Auditing & Accountability Journal*, 21(3), 427–454; and Herman Aguinis (2019) *Performance management for dummies*, Hoboken, NJ: John Wiley & Sons.

3   See Hugh Southey, Amanda Weston, Jude Bunting and Raj Desai (2017) *Judicial review: A practical guide*, Bristol: Jordans; and Raphael Hogarth (2020) *Judicial review*, London: Institute for Government.

4   In a committee hearing on 5 June 2014. See Public Accounts Committee (2014) *Major projects authority*, 16 July. The programme was called a shambles by Frank Field MP, chair of the Work and Pensions Select Committee, on the publication of the National Audit Office's (2018) report *Rolling out universal credit*, 15 June.

5   In the National Audit Office's (2016) *Report on the Department for Education's financial statements 2014–15*, Comptroller and Auditor General Amyas Morse said: 'Providing Parliament with a clear view of academy trusts' spending is a vital part of the Department for Education's work, yet it is failing to do this.'

6   Eleanor Busby (2016) 'Academy chain spends £440,000 on deals with firms run by CEO and his daughter', *Times Educational Supplement*, 24 October.

7   National Audit Office (2018) *PFI and PF2*, 18 January.

8   Marc Hertogh and Richard Kirkham (eds) (2018) *Research handbook on the ombudsman*, Cheltenham: Edward Elgar.

9   Ed Hammond (2018) *Local Public Accounts Committees – Discussion paper*, London: Centre for Governance and Scrutiny. In September 2018, Labour MP Andrew Gwynne supported the establishment of Local Public Accounts Committees 'to improve local government spending decisions', as did Meg Hillier MP, then chair of the Public Accounts Committee. See Dominic Brady (2018) 'PAC chair seeking ways to beef up local government spending scrutiny', *Public Finance*, 17 October. The Audit Commission inspected and audited local government in England between 1983 and 2015, when it was abolished. A history of its first 25 years can be found in Duncan Campbell-Smith (2008) *Follow the money: The Audit Commission, public money and the management of public services*, London: Allen Lane.

10   For information about UN finances, see United Nations Association (2017) *UN briefings: The UN's finances*, 7 July, and UN Resolution 73/271, passed on 22 December 2018. In 2021, the UN Board of Auditors comprised auditors from Germany, China and Chile (www.un.org/en/auditors/board/index.shtml).

11   See Jo Casebourne (2014) *Why motivation matters in public sector innovation*, London: Nesta.

12   Tiffany Ito, Jeff Larsen, Kyle Smith and John Cacioppo (1998) 'Negative information weighs more heavily on the brain: The negativity bias in evaluative categorizations', *Journal of Personality and Social Psychology*, 75(4), 887–900.

13   Keith Wheldall and Frank Merrett (2017) *Positive teaching: The behavioural approach*, London: Routledge.

14   See UNESCO Institute for Statistics (no date) 'How much does your country invest in R&D?'. EU R&D expenditure represents 2.2 per cent

of overall GDP: Eurostat (2020) 'R & D expenditure'. The other 12 companies are Alphabet, Volkswagen, Samsung, Microsoft, Huawei, Intel, Apple, Roche, Johnson & Johnson, Daimler, Merck and Toyota, according to data in Strategy&'s 2018 Global Innovation 1000 Study and the EU's 2018 Industrial R&D Investment Scorecard. See Nick Skillicorn (2019) 'Top 1000 companies that spend the most on Research & Development', Idea to Value.

15 Vijay Govindarajan and Srikanth Srinivas (2013) 'The innovation mindset in action: 3M corporation', *Harvard Business Review*, 6 August.

16 Juan Alcacer, Tarun Khanna and Christine Snively (2014) 'The rise and fall of Nokia', *Harvard Business Review*, 6 January.

17 Michael Mankins (2017) 'Great companies obsess over productivity, not efficiency', *Harvard Business Review*, 1 March.

18 As reported in the *Financial Times* (2021) 'Global MBA ranking 2021'.

19 *The Economist* (2019) 'The next business revolution', 2 November.

20 An exception is Marcial Bóo and Alexander Stevenson (2015) *The public sector fox: Twelve ways to become a brilliant public sector manager*, Kibworth Beauchamp: Matador.

21 Jake Beech, Simon Bottery, Anita Charlesworth, Harry Evans, Ben Gershlick, Nina Hemmings et al (2019) *Closing the gap: Key areas for action on the health and care workforce*, London: The Health Foundation, The King's Fund, Nuffield Foundation.

22 Jan-Erik Lane (2000) *New public management*, Abingdon: Routledge.

23 Ben Zaranko (2020) 'The outlook for public spending', Institute for Fiscal Studies, 26 February, shows a real-terms decline in spending from 2010−11 to 2020−21 of over 30 per cent in transport, over 20 per cent in justice and over 10 per cent to government departments including the Home Office, HM Revenue and Customs, Department for Digital, Culture, Media and Sport and Department for Environment, Food & Rural Affairs.

Chapter 7

1 Outlined by Stanley Milgram (1970) 'The experience of living in cities: A psychological analysis', in F. Korten, S. Cook and J. Lacey (eds) *Psychology and the problems of society*, Washington, DC: American Psychological Association, pp 152–73.

2 David McMillan and David Chavis (1986) 'Sense of community: A definition and theory', *Journal of Community Psychology*, 14(1), 6–23. These issues are also examined in Robert Putnam (2001) *Bowling alone: The collapse and revival of American community*, New York: Simon & Schuster.

3 Peter Johnson, Pamela Robinson and Simone Philpot (2020) 'Type, tweet, tap, and pass: How smart city technology is creating a transactional citizen', *Government Information Quarterly*, 37(1), January.

4 Electoral Commission (2019) *Results and turnout at the 2017 UK general election*; House of Commons (2019) *General Election 2017: Full results and analysis*.

5   Lisa Hill (2004) 'Compulsory voting in Australia: A basis for a "best practice" regime', *Federal Law Review*, 32(3), 479–97.

6   For an exposition of the arguments, see Jason Brennan and Lisa Hill (2014) *Compulsory voting: For and against*, Cambridge: Cambridge University Press; and Anthoula Malkopoulou (2014) *The history of compulsory voting in Europe: Democracy's duty?*, Abingdon: Routledge.

7   Postal voting took place across the world through the COVID-19 pandemic and withstood intense scrutiny, particularly in the November 2019 US elections. See also Robert Krimmer, Melanie Volkamer, Veronique Cortier, Rajeev Goré, Manik Hapsara, Uwe Serdulk and David Duenas-Cid (eds) (2018) *Electronic voting: Third International Joint Conference, E-Vote-ID 2018, Bregenz, Austria, October 2–5, 2018, Proceedings*, Cham: Springer.

8   See Elvis Bisong Tambe (2020) 'Why do the poor and less educated vote more? Explaining the reverse relationship between socio-economic status and turnout in Africa', African Politics Conference (www.semanticscholar. org/paper/Why-Do-the-Poor-and-Less-Educated-Vote-More-the-and-Tambe/fe9bf3b075cb9905b0f13bfdc87050597ed18931#paper-header).

9   Derek Wall (2010) *The no-nonsense guide to green politics*, Oxford: New Internationalist.

10 United Nations (2017) *Volunteers count: Their work deserves to be counted*, 2 November.

11 According to the National Council of Voluntary Organisations (2020) 'How many people volunteer and what do they do?', *UK Civil Society Almanac 2020*.

12 This comprises the £24 billion output of formal volunteers, the £45 billion output of informal volunteers and the estimated £70 billion 'wellbeing value' accrued to volunteers themselves. Figures are from the Office for National Statistics, Volunteering England and the Cabinet Office, quoted by Matt Hill (2014) 'It's the economic value stupid. But is volunteering worth £100 billion a year?', NCVO, 26 June.

13 International Volunteer Day was adopted by the UN through Resolution A/RES/40/212 on 17 December 1985. It is generally held on 5 December each year.

14 The US comes first in a combined index of charitable giving, volunteering and helping strangers. The countries where over 65 per cent of people give money are Myanmar, the UK, Malta, Thailand, the Netherlands, Indonesia, Ireland, Australia and New Zealand. See Charities Aid Foundation (2019) *World Giving Index 2019: 10 years of giving trends*, October. Other UK figures in this section are from Charities Aid Foundation (2019) *UK giving 2019: An overview of charitable giving in the UK*, May.

15 Larry Dossey (2018) 'The helper's high', *Explore*, 14(6), November, 393–9; Corporation for National and Community Service (2007) *The health benefits of volunteering: A review of recent research*, Washington, DC: Office of Research and Policy Development.

16 See Jeni Warburton (2003) 'Out of the generosity of your heart: Are we creating active citizens through compulsory volunteer programmes for

young people in Australia?', *Social Policy Administration*, 37(7), 772–86; Piret Tõnurist and Laidi Surva (2013) 'Is volunteering always voluntary? Between compulsion and coercion in co-production', *VOLUNTAS: International Journal of Voluntary and Non-profit Organizations*, 28, 223–47.

[17] The Conservative Party's 2019 election manifesto proposed requiring public sector employers and companies with more than 250 employees to give staff up to three days a year off for voluntary work. See also Jon Yates (2021) *Fractured: Why our societies are coming apart and how we put them back together again*, Manchester: HarperNorth. Mark Carney (2021) *Value(s): Building a better world for all*, Glasgow: William Collins, argues that individuals have a role in responding to globalisation so that communities can build 'the supporting infrastructure for the two great re-wirings of our economies: the digital revolution and the sustainable transformation. This requires credible, predicable regulatory policies. … And it must include a series of measures to empower people to participate fully in the economy' (p 13).

[18] Jean-Jacques Rousseau (1762) *The social contract*, Constitution Society.

Conclusion

[1] On 17 February 2021, Scott Morrison said that Facebook's decision to withdraw its news service from Australia in response to proposed legislation 'will only confirm the concerns that an increasing number of countries are expressing about the behaviour of Big Tech companies who think they are bigger than governments and that the rules should not apply to them'. Speaking at the UN's Climate Action Summit on 23 September 2019, Greta Thunberg said: 'For more than 30 years, the science has been crystal clear. How dare you continue to look away and come here saying that you're doing enough, when the politics and solutions needed are still nowhere in sight.'

[2] Arundhati Roy said at the World Social Forum in Mumbai on 16 January 2004: 'Poor countries that are geo-politically of strategic value to Empire, or have a "market" of any size, or infrastructure that can be privatised, or, God forbid, natural resources of value – oil, gold, diamonds, cobalt, coal – must do as they're told, or become military targets. Those with the greatest reserves of natural wealth are most at risk. Unless they surrender their resources willingly to the corporate machine, civil unrest will be fomented, or war will be waged.'

[3] On 24 December 2020, Boris Johnson said: 'It is four and a half years since the British people voted to take back control of their money, their borders, their laws, and their waters and to leave the European Union. … We have taken back control of laws and our destiny. We have taken back control of every jot and title of our regulation. In a way that is complete and unfettered. … British laws will be made solely by the British Parliament. Interpreted by UK judges sitting in UK courts' (see www.gov. uk/government/speeches/prime-ministers-statement-on-eu-negotiations-24-december-2020).

Notes

4   The Belarusian election of 9 August 2020 returned Alexander Lukashenko to the presidency with 80 per cent of the vote, although fraud was alleged by many countries, including the EU. The 6 September 2020 Hong Kong elections were postponed by Chief Executive Carrie Lam, with 12 opposition candidates banned from standing, and many claiming that the move was to stifle the pro-democracy opposition. The 17–19 September 2021 Russian elections took place after many opposition candidates, in particular Alexei Navalny, had been removed from the ballot, exiled or jailed. Vladimir Putin's party won 50 per cent of the vote, although there were widespread reports of fraud. In Myanmar, the army ousted democratic politicians in a coup on 1 February 2021. The subsequent protests led to the death of over 800 people and the detention of over 4,000.

5   Plato (2007) *The republic*, London: Penguin Classics; Alexander Hamilton, James Madison and John Jay (1987) *The federalist papers*, London: Penguin Classics; Max Weber (2019) *Economy and society*, Cambridge, MA: Harvard University Press.

6   Thomas Kuhn (1970) *The structure of scientific revolutions*, Chicago, IL: University of Chicago Press, noted that: 'Political revolutions are inaugurated by a growing sense, often restricted to a segment of the political community, that existing institutions have ceased adequately to meet the problems posed by an environment that they have in part created' (p 92).

Index

References to figures are in *italics*. References to notes show both the page number and note number (146n6).